HOW TO STUDY LITERATURE
General Editors: John Peck and Ma

HOW TO STUDY AN E. M. FORSTER NOVEL

IN THE SAME SERIES

How to Study a Novel   *John Peck*
Literary Terms and Criticism   *John Peck and Martin Coyle*
How to Study a Shakespeare Play   *John Peck and Martin Coyle*
How to Begin Studying Literature   *Nicholas Marsh*
How to Study a Jane Austen Novel   *Vivien Jones*
How to Study a Thomas Hardy Novel   *John Peck*
How to Study a D. H. Lawrence Novel   *Nigel Messenger*
How to Study a Charles Dickens Novel   *Keith Selby*
How to Study a Joseph Conrad Novel   *Brian Spittles*
How to Study a Renaissance Play   *Chris Coles*
How to Study Modern Drama   *Kenneth Pickering*
How to Study a Poet   *John Peck*
How to Study Chaucer   *Rob Pope*
How to Study Romantic Poetry   *Paul O'Flinn*
How to Study Modern Poetry   *Tony Curtis*

IN PREPARATION

How to Study a James Joyce Novel   *Chris Coles*

HOW TO STUDY AN E. M. FORSTER NOVEL

Nigel Messenger

MACMILLAN

823 FOR

52257

First published 1991

Published by
MACMILLAN EDUCATION LTD
Houndmills, Basingstoke, Hampshire RG21 2XS
and London
Companies and representatives
throughout the world

Filmset by Wearside Tradespools, Fulwell, Sunderland
Printed in Hong Kong

British Library Cataloguing in Publication Data
Messenger, Nigel
    How to study an E. M. Forster novel.
    1. Fiction in English. Forster, E. M. (Edward Morgan),
    1879–1970 – Critical studies
    I. Title
    823.912
    ISBN 0–333–49155–6

To
Jenny, Marcus, Timothy and Abigail

Contents

General Editors' preface

Everybody who studies literature, either for an examination or simply for pleasure, experiences the same problem: how to understand and respond to the text. As every student of literature knows, it is perfectly possible to read a book over and over again and yet still feel baffled and at a loss as to what to say about it. One answer to this problem, of course, is to accept someone else's view of the text, but how much more rewarding it would be if you could work out your own critical response to any book you choose or are required to study.

The aim of this series is to help you develop your critical skills by offering practical advice about how to read, understand and analyse literature. Each volume provides you with a clear method of study so that you can see how to set about tackling texts on your own. While the authors of each volume approach the problem in a different way, every book in the series attempts to provide you with some broad ideas about the kind of texts you are likely to be studying and some broad ideas about how to think about literature; each volume then shows you how to apply these ideas in a way which should help you construct your own analysis and interpretation. Unlike most critical books, therefore, the books in this series do not simply convey someone else's thinking about a text, but encourage you and show you how to think about a text for yourself.

Each book is written with an awareness that you are likely to be preparing for an examination, and therefore practical advice is given not only on how to understand and analyse literature, but also on how to organise a written response. Our hope is that, although these books are intended to serve a practical purpose, they may also enrich your enjoyment of literature by making you a more confident reader, alert to the interest and pleasure to be derived from literary texts.

John Peck
Martin Coyle

Acknowledgements

I should like to thank my colleagues in the Humanities Department at Oxford Polytechnic for helping me in so many ways, and past students who have shared their readings of Forster with me. In particular I owe a special debt to Charles Smith at the Computer Centre who patiently instructed me in the skills of word-processing. He has made the writing of this book much less arduous than it would otherwise have been.

I should also like to express my gratitude to the general editors of this series. They have been generous with their encouragement, and have supervised this book at every stage with tactful vigilance.

1
Studying Forster:
some ideas to get you started

Working on a novelist for a course or exam is not the same as reading for simple enjoyment although, hopefully, a good deal of lasting pleasure can be derived from studying fictions as 'literary texts'. Still, whatever other motives a serious author may have, novels are written with entertainment in mind. Novelists don't want to be dreary and dull, and don't set out expecting their work to be put on examination syllabuses, so I think the best way to start is by reading your text through once, carefully but not too solemnly, as you would any other novel, and then try to record your own reading experience as honestly as you can. Studying a book is a rather different process from reading for pleasure because you have to keep at it longer in a systematic way and be prepared to go beyond first impressions – but first impressions are still important. There will always be critics around to tell you what they think but, right from the start, try and get into the argument yourself, however inadequate you may feel, before becoming too influenced by other people's ideas. Let us suppose, then, that you have just finished reading the Forster novel that you have to study; try and make some assessment of the experience you have had by jotting down your first impressions. Do this now before you move on to the next section.

What kind of a novelist is E. M. Forster?

If your experience of reading Forster has been anything like mine, you may well have finished your chosen text with mixed feelings. On the one hand, you might feel rather reassured. Forster doesn't seem *that* difficult; indeed, you could be wondering what all the fuss is about. The novel is set in the past, but not so far back that it seems necessary to discover more about the culture and society in which it is set, as you would have to if you were faced with an eighteenth-century novel, or even one by Dickens. On the other hand, Forster doesn't seem to be so devastatingly experimental and complex in a 'modern' way either; the language and structure of the text do not present the obvious difficulties of a fiction by, say, James Joyce or Virginia Woolf. The 'feel' of the book is rather conventional and old-fashioned. Also the scale is unambitious and domestic. Still, there is obvious pleasure to be got from reading a good story presented in an orthodox manner which offers us plausible characters which we can identify with, or dislike.

With a little bit more reflection, however, you might become more uneasy. You've read the story all right, but you can't be too sure that you have got the point. Maybe the ending threw you a bit; you were expecting it to round things off neatly, but then it suddenly moved away in an unexpected direction in a manner that makes you want to go back and see what it is that you've missed. Or what seemed initially to be so safe and solid turns out not to be solid at all. You might have registered sudden unexpected turns and twists in the plot that seem unnecessarily abrupt or abitrary: implausible marriages or sudden deaths that serve to remind you that you are reading a book and not just observing life. Most novels work around plot coincidences, but Forster seems to enjoy making them obvious and, by doing so, emphasising the pattern in his texts. Another thing you may have noticed is that although your novel starts in a humdrum, low key, domestic manner, it doesn't stay that way for long. The story might seem 'real' in that it is keeping to the ordinary surface of life, but then the most 'unreal' passion or violence will keep breaking through to disrupt – even temporarily destroy – the social order in the novel that seemed so safe and stable. These outbursts are wildly improbable at one level, yet can also be seen as the only true reality at another. So you might conclude that your novel is not so straightforward as it appeared at first. One sort of writing expressing a conventional, material reality keeps dissolving into another that is poetic, personal, even visionary. Once you have picked up this dissonance in Forster's view of the world, he becomes a rather mysterious writer – or a confusing, muddled one.

Forster in context

There is a tendency to attribute the characteristics of writers to their own personal quirks, and their own unique vision of the world. There is no doubt that every writer is distinctive, but more factors than individual talent are at work when any writer writes anything. What is true for writers is true for readers also. The basis of this book is close reading because 'studying Forster' begins and ends with the texts themselves. But we bring to any text what we know, and there are things about Forster that are helpful to know before we get started, so I'm going to place Forster's novels in three overlapping contexts, quickly and briefly. Whatever texts you are studying, I think you will find the information useful.

The historical context

Forster is an Edwardian novelist; all his novels were written before the First World War with the exception of his most famous, *A Passage to India* (1924) and that was partially drafted before 1914. The Edwardian period is deceptively close to us and has been invested with a particular kind of glamour. It was the period when Britain's imperial power was at its grandest and most extensive; in retrospect, it seems a time of unrivalled peace and prosperity before the horrors of the trenches, and all the atrocities that were to follow during the rest of the twentieth century. Many cultural factors have combined to give us an image of the Edwardian period as a time of seeming stability, charm and innocence.

Forster's novels have played their part in this nostalgia through the manner in which they have been marketed and reproduced. Through films especially, many readers come to Forster for the first time with very clear assumptions of what the texts are like and what they contain; the impression is that Forster's fictional world is going to be one of pretty girls in white muslin, vicars, tea parties and beautiful scenery. 'Forster' becomes a kind of racier Jane Austen in Edwardian dress. While some of this is not entirely untrue, there is a lot that is, and the reader should be aware of the distortion. In fact, the Edwardian period was one of great extremes of affluence and poverty. While the upper classes flourished and lived lives of comfortable leisure, their prosperity depended on large investments abroad and a huge labour force at home. The lower classes led lives of constrained respectability or unrelieved squalor in the big cities that had grown up during the nineteenth century. The Edwardian period was not that calm and peaceful; indeed, in some ways it was remarkably like our own time – an odd mixture of complacency and panic. There were riots, strikes, campaigns of civil disobedience, troubles in Ireland, and an arms race with Imperial Germany. Forster may not often confront the social inequalities and tensions of the Edwardian period directly in his fiction, but they are an important context in which his work was written, and should be remembered when his novels are read.

The social and political context

Forster was a middle class, liberal intellectual and this makes him particularly alert to the social inequalities of the time and the contradictions in his position. To put it simply, he was sensitive, clever and quite wealthy; while he enjoyed his class privileges, he was also well aware of the injustices that made them possible. The politics and philosophy of liberalism, with its stress on freedom and democracy, had been dynamic and progressive throughout the Victorian period, and had effected reforms as well as making the middle classes powerful. In the Edwardian period that followed, this liberal consensus was threatened by a number of new pressures, especially the challenge of socialism, and began to break up. It became increasingly difficult for liberalism as a political philosophy to defend middle-class power and also be socially progressive. In order to maintain their authority, liberal politicians had to strengthen the state and became less responsive to minority demands and social injustices. This offended many liberal intellectuals.

As a writer, Forster reflects this crisis of confidence and conscience. He knew the middle class intimately from the inside, and respected its energy and its liberal traditions. He also appreciated the security and support that it gave him. However, he also viewed the development of a modern capitalist state with some alarm for it threatened the liberties of the individual, depressed the poor and despoiled the environment in ways he felt were unacceptable. So, because of his class position, we have in Forster a writer with divided loyalties. Part of him yearned for some radical transformation of society so that the individual could experience a freedom and fulfilment not possible in a modern industrial state, but he was also aware that his own comfort, security and cultural values would be threatened, very possibly destroyed, by such a change. This dilemma goes some way to explaining the strains and stresses in Forster's novels as he sought to find a satisfactory compromise between the conflicting demands of individual desire and social conformity. His novels provide a record of this struggle.

The personal context

Rather like his books, Forster's own life is a fascinating mixture of conformity and discreet nonconformity. He was a homosexual. I intend to discuss some of the artistic implications of this in my next chapter. I will just say here that, however much he might have been a social insider because of his class privileges, his homosexuality inevitably meant that he was also secretly alienated from society in some important respects. It enabled him to view his class more critically than he might otherwise have done, and gave him a social curiosity about the lives of those outside his class and culture. It made him sensitive to class power and class division, and also goes some way to explain his Utopian yearnings for a transformed society. Apart from this decisive but private influence, Forster's life history is both typical and rather unusual for one of his background. Before he was ten, he had received a legacy from his great-aunt that gave him financial security for the rest of his life. Public school and Cambridge were followed by genteel travels in the Mediterranean, lecturing, tutoring, and, of course, writing. All this is quite unexceptional for a cultured, public spirited man of his class at this time.

As the novels received recognition, so Forster's public reputation rose, and in the later part of his life he became a venerable institution as a Fellow at King's College, Cambridge. Other parts of his biography show more marginal, unconforming inclinations. He was associated with the Bloomsbury Group, that unconventional artistic set, and had other connections with

London literary Bohemia. He served with the Red Cross in Egypt during the First World War and made two long visits to India, the second of which was spent as a private secretary to a Maharajah of an Indian state. This shows more cosmopolitan interests and provided Forster with opportunities for seeing British power and rule operating in other parts of the world. Forster writes from within the English middle class and this gives confidence and urbanity to his style, but he always provides other cultural and class contexts from which we can view it.

What can all this tell us about Forster's novels?

Well, I hope you have already begun to draw some conclusions for yourself. It is clear that Forster's novels are marked by pressures and conflicts that extend beyond his personal life to his class and his time. They both conform to accepted literary expectations and beliefs about social reality inherited from the great Victorian novelists while simultaneously challenging them. Friends in the Bloomsbury Group nicknamed Forster 'the taupe', which means the mole. It seems to sum up the canny, secretive side of Forster rather well; the manner in which he can move around 'underground', so to speak, undermining prejudices and assumptions while staying safe and protected himself.

I think you will find that Forster has wonderful gifts for social comedy in all his novels, and these are what we tend to notice first. Forster has been prized for his wisdom, his humane social views and his depiction of a stable, complacent, suburban world that has gone for ever. As we have seen, he is eminently qualified for that. But there is another side to his creative personality. The paradox is well captured by his friend and fellow novelist, Virginia Woolf, when she wrote in an essay about his novels that he was 'always constrained to build the cage – society in all its intricacy and triviality – before he can free the prisoner' ('The Novels of E. M. Forster', *Collected Essays*, vol. 1). This other side of Forster, wishing to 'free the prisoner', struggles to discover and articulate the potential glory in life and art, and to reject the modern world for what he feels is a more authentic, pre-industrial past. He concerns himself in his novels with the hazards and rewards awaiting those brave enough to follow the impulses of their hearts, resisting the blandishments of safe, social conformity. So Forster negotiates between contrary impulses and different 'layers' of reality in his fiction, and, as readers, we need to be alert to these sudden switches and changes. More simply, we can expect as we read a Forster novel to find a constant tension between the need to conform to society and a desire to break free of it. Hopefully, the contexts I have provided here suggest an explanation for this and for why Forster is the kind of novelist that he is.

2

The Private Forster: an analysis of *Maurice* (1913–14)

I want to start with something of a false start. Forster wrote *Maurice* after all his other novels with the exception of *A Passage to India*. It is not a great novel, perhaps not even a very good one. The plot is simple, all the characters save one undeveloped, the fictional texture sketchy and thin. Critics are more or less unanimous that Forster's characteristic strengths only appear fitfully. Consequently, it is unlikely to appear on an exam syllabus. Why then, you might ask, are we bothering to look at it at all? Well, because I think it will give us some insight into Forster's problems and difficulties both as a man and a writer. The novel's obvious weakness will be helpful, I think, in defining the nature of Forster's strengths in the 'official' novels that do get put on exam syllabuses. I say 'official' because *Maurice* was a clandestine work that Forster wrote for himself and a few friends when he felt very unhappy and 'dried-up' as a writer. It was not intended for publication; had it been, it would, no doubt, have been a different sort of book, but that would have meant Forster being a different sort of man. A brief summary of the story will make Forster's difficulties very clear. When studying any fiction this is always the first step.

1 *After reading the novel, think about the story and what kind of pattern you can see in the text*

Maurice Hall is the only son of a respectable Edwardian family. His home for most of the novel is middle-class, London suburbia where he lives with his widowed mother and his two sisters. After public school and Cambridge, he seems destined for an unexceptional life as a stockbroker in the family firm. However, though to outer appearances an entirely conventional business man whose career does indeed take the predictable route, Maurice is a homosexual. Most of the novel explores his slow discovery of this fact, the effect that it has on his private life, and how, finally, it transforms his existence.

After briefly following Maurice through his school days, the substance of the novel examines his relationship with two contrasting lovers. Maurice meets Clive Durham, a young squire, at Cambridge; they fall in love and have an intense, lyrical, platonic relationship that lasts for three years. Then, quite suddenly, Clive experiences an emotional change and reverts to 'normal' sexual feeling. He marries and takes up his role as pillar of the local community. Maurice is devastated. Full of sexual guilt and emotional self-loathing, he seeks a cure for his condition without any success. Matters are brought to a crisis on a visit Maurice makes to Penge, Clive's country house. He has a sexual liaison with Alex Scudder, a gamekeeper on the estate. After the initial revulsion, fear and consequent antagonism between this socially ill-matched pair, Maurice persuades Alex to give up his plans to emigrate and live with him outside respectable society. The book ends with Maurice telling Clive of his new love before beginning his life as a social outlaw.

The pattern of this story is a very familiar one. It is an 'education' novel, that is one that shows the growth and development of a young person from childhood to maturity. Such novels are always episodic, take the shape of a life and end on a note of resolution. The plot follows the fortunes of the main character who is always at odds with society in some way. After misfortunes and difficulties of various kinds the hero or heroine make crucial discoveries about themselves and their society, and so are finally able to enter into some defining role in that society. Sometimes this is achieved through finding a vocation; more usually it is through marriage or finding acceptance into a family. When the form of Forster's novel is outlined in this way, the difficulties become apparent immediately. The heterosexual assumptions behind this form of mainstream fiction where the main character must learn to adjust to society are not designed to embody Forster's very personal subject matter. There is no way in which Maurice could be integrated back into society because his sexual nature is seen as profoundly *anti*-social. In some ways, Clive's story is the conventional one; Maurice's homosexual desire points in quite a different direction and so there are no ready-made fictional conventions that help Forster articulate it convincingly.

As regards its subject matter, you might feel that Forster's story is mild enough; hardly worth hiding away in a drawer unpublished until 1971, a year after his death. We need to remind ourselves here, however, of the historical context in which it was written. The Edwardian period was morally very repressive, in some ways far more so than the Victorian age that preceded it, and homosexuals in particular had to live under the shadow of Oscar Wilde's disgrace. He had been tried and imprisoned for homosexuality in 1895, when Forster was sixteen. Practising homosexuals were regarded as criminal, liable both to imprisonment if convicted but also blackmail. There was no possibility of Forster publishing this novel in England at the time it was written. Even the widespread knowledge of its existence would have been sufficient to destroy his public career as journalist, academic and liberal sage. *Maurice* is a transparent exercise in personal therapy and wish-fulfilment – it is dedicated to 'a happier year' – and such naked expressions of personal desire and despair rarely make successful works of literature. They can be very informative about the writer, however, revealing those private concerns that must be disguised, reformed or overlaid in more public statements. Reading *Maurice* will not provide an instant understanding of Forster's gifts, but it may give us a helpful access to them.

With these thoughts in mind, let us begin to examine the novel a little more closely. It is clear that Maurice is the main character and the best way forward is to take a passage near the beginning of the book that features him and seems important. This is the next step, so:

2   *Select a short passage featuring one of the main characters and try to build upon the ideas you have established so far*

I have chosen a passage in the third chapter depicting Maurice's

life at public school (page references to the novel relate to the
Penguin edition, 1972).

Where all is obscure and unrealised the best similitude is a
dream. Maurice had two dreams at school; they will interpret
him.

In the first dream he felt very cross. He was playing football
against a nondescript whose existence he resented. He made
an effort and the nondescript turned into George, that garden
boy. But he had to be careful or it would reappear. George
headed down the field towards him, naked and jumping over
the woodstacks. 'I shall go mad if he turns wrong now,' said
Maurice, and just as they collared this happened, and a brutal
disappointment woke him up. He did not connect it with Mr
Dulce's homily still less with his second dream, but he thought
he was going to be ill, and afterwards that it was somehow a
punishment for something.

The second dream is more difficult to convey. Nothing
happened. He scarcely saw a face, scarcely heard a voice say,
'That is your friend,' and then it was over, having filled him
with beauty and taught him tenderness. He could die for such
a friend, he would allow such a friend to die for him; they
would make any sacrifice for each other, and count the world
nothing, neither death nor distance nor crossness could part
them, because 'this is my friend.' Soon afterwards he was
confirmed and tried to persuade himself that the friend must
be Christ. But Christ has a mangy beard. Was he a Greek god,
such as illustrates the classical dictionary? More probable, but
most probably he was just a man. Maurice forbore to define
his dream further. (pp. 25–6)

When you wish to examine a passage like this with a little more
attention than merely casual reading, it is best if you have a plan.
This will enable you to structure your study, give it purpose and
direction. I shall have more to say about this in my next chapter.
Just for the moment, let's concentrate on finding some sort of
conflict or tension in the passage. Conflict is essential for any
narrative because, bluntly, without conflicts of some kind, no
story has dramatic interest or psychological curiosity. Stories are
rather like puzzles; part of the pleasure for a reader is learning
what the problems are, how the author intends to solve them,

and then, whether the solution satisfies us, the readers. When we find conflicts or tensions in one passage that seem important to the understanding of a character, we can be sure that they can be found elsewhere: indeed, that they help shape the book as a whole. That's why it's helpful to build up our study of a novel from detailed analyses of short passages.

Maurice's schooldays are very skimpily covered. The fact that Forster makes these two dreams the most important event of his schooldays is in itself a comment on the failure of his formal education to engage with his inner development. The two dreams are contrasting and seem to express conflicting emotional needs within Maurice. One dream is of male conflict, upsetting, exciting but rather rough, and leaves him feeling guilty. The other is very lyrical, emotional and mysterious. Maurice's vision of this ideal friend has a haunting quality that he can't define or fit into his everyday experience.

The first dream is physical and clearly sexual in nature. We remember from the previous chapter how upset Maurice had been when he learnt of the departure of George, the garden boy, on his return home from prep school. The dream draws on happy memories of their childhood games in and around the woodstacks. But now they are naked and George's identity keeps melting into a 'nondescript', an objectification of an impersonal need. The collaring or wrestling seems to be a displaced expression, or metaphor, for a needed sexual contact that is resented, hence the 'crossness'. The term 'nondescript' seems to imply that this shadowy figure is, like George, from the lower orders, so there is a class reaction as well as sexual guilt in the 'brutal disappointment' when he 'turns wrong'. There is a sense of let-down and disability, too, in 'he thought he was going to be ill'. 'Turns wrong' suggests the guilty frustration of a wish that is desired but also feared. This explains Maurice's exhaustion and fear of punishment when he wakes up. The narrator's comment that he does not connect this experience with his old teacher's lecture on the facts of life clearly implies a connection but not one that the conventional Mr Dulce would recognise.

The second dream, by contrast, is full of ill-defined yearnings that have a romantic and religious intensity, based on the need for an ideal friend whose presence is scarcely palpable. This figure is not a 'nondescript' but vague in other ways, as platonic as the other was physical. If the first dream was a 'brutal disappointment' and fearfully rejected, this is full of self-sacrificing ardour and nobility. There are images of martyrdom – 'He could die for such a friend ... they would make any sacrifice for each other' – and a rejection of all worldly things to be at one with the friend. There is a Biblical elevation in the phrasing of this second passage too: '... count the world nothing, neither death nor distance nor crossness could part them ...'. Finally, there's another shift of tone at the end of the passage into comic bathos as Maurice attempts to locate and embody his vision in the inadequate orthodoxies of his religious training and education. The ideal friend is first Christ, disqualified because of his 'mangy beard', then a Greek god, and finally 'just a man' as Maurice shies away from the implications of his dream.

I think that Forster cleverly manages in all this to suggest the confused and limited nature of his hero's self-awareness; Maurice is seen as a not very bright late Victorian public schoolboy reaching out for needs that he can't identify or articulate very well. The passage seems important because at the outset of the book it clearly describes the divided nature of Maurice's secret life. It suggests to me that the book is going to concern itself with Maurice's search for his 'ideal friend' and with the need to integrate his divided nature.

Let us move on and examine another passage further into the book.

3 Select a second passage for discussion

I've chosen a passage in Part 2, Chapter 16, when Maurice, now aware of his sexual nature and consciously in love with Clive, visits him at Penge, the family home.

'Pippa, does Mr Hall know his room?'
'The Blue Room, mamma.'
'The one with no fireplace,' called Clive. 'Show him up.' He was seeing off some callers.

Miss Durham passed Maurice on to the butler. They went up a side staircase, Maurice saw the main flight to the right, and wondered whether he was being slighted. His room was small, furnished cheaply. It had no outlook. As he knelt down to unpack, a feeling of Sunnington came over him, and he determined, while he was at Penge, to work through all his clothes. They shouldn't suppose he was unfashionable; he was as good as anyone. But he had scarcely reached this conclusion when Clive rushed in with the sunlight behind him. 'Maurice, I shall kiss you,' he said, and did so.

'Where – what's through there?'

'Our study – ' He was laughing, his expression wild and radiant.

'Oh, so that's why – '

'Maurice! Maurice! You've actually come. You're here. This place'll never seem the same again, I shall love it at last.'

'It's jolly for me coming,' said Maurice chokily: the sudden rush of joy made his head swim.

'Go on unpacking. So I arranged it on purpose. We're up this staircase by ourselves. It's as like college as I could manage.'

'It's better.'

'I really feel it will be.'

There was a knock on the passage door. Maurice started, but Clive though still sitting on his shoulder said 'Come in!' indifferently. A house maid entered with hot water.

(pp. 82–3)

This passage shows something of Maurice's arrival, his formal reception and then his joy when greeted by Clive privately in his room. The tension here is between Maurice's social insecurity in a much grander house than his own suburban home and then his relief at the warmth of Clive's greeting.

There is a social distance in the formality of address at the beginning of the passage. Clive's sister 'passes' Maurice to the butler rather like a parcel. He is disturbed at being taken up a side staircase instead of the main one, and at the meagre furnishings of his room. Remembering his public schooldays, Maurice resolves to keep up appearances in this hostile environment. With the sun shining behind him, Clive's sudden reappearance through the connecting door is miraculous; it belongs to a different order of reality. He is idealised and seen as some kind of transfigured angel, 'wild and radiant'. The emotional directness of his greeting is in shocking contrast to the impersonality of Maurice's arrival. Clive also provides the reason for the choice of the spartan Blue Room: it is as much like a college staircase as possible so they can be near each other and privately enclosed. The effect of this on Maurice is overwhelming; his head swims with a 'sudden rush of joy' and he can only respond inarticulately with the language of a schoolboy. The disturbance of the maid is a reminder of the social reality outside the Blue Room. Clive is at home; Maurice is not.

This is the first time that we see the pair together outside the privileged environment of Cambridge where their love had flourished. I think we are given a sense that their relationship won't be easy to maintain in the outside world. They need to create a private space as much like Cambridge as possible and lead a double life. Secret joy has to be concealed in social conformity. This must be a source of stress once the raptures of first love have passed and, added to the social differences between them, make for difficulties. Clive has imported a private fantasy world into his conventional social world. Maurice's role in this is uncomfortable: he is a privileged insider through his emotional intimacy with Clive and yet, because of his class, something of an outsider simultaneously. It is not surprising that the affair is doomed and that eventually Clive will be reclaimed by his class for his destined role in the social order. Even at this stage we can see Forster qualifying ecstasy with ominous warning signs.

I'd now like to look at a passage where Maurice, deserted by Clive, is trying to come to terms with his homosexuality on his own.

4   Select a third passage for discussion

When the fellow had gone he faced the truth. His feeling for Dickie required a very primitive name. He would have sentimentalized once and called it adoration, but the habit of honesty had grown strong. What a stoat he had been! Poor little Dickie! He saw the boy leaping from his embrace, to smash through the window and break his limbs, or yelling like a maniac until help came. He saw the police –

'Lust.' He said the word out loud.

Lust is negligible when absent. In the calm of his office Maurice expected to subdue it, now that he had found its

name. His mind, ever practical, wasted no time in theological
despair, but advanced to the grindstone. He had been forewarned, and therefore forearmed, and had only to keep away
from boys and young men to ensure success. Yes, from other
young men. Certain obscurities of the last six months became
clear. For example, a pupil at the Settlement – He wrinkled
his nose, as one who needs no further proof. The feeling that
can impel a gentleman towards a person of lower class stands
self-condemned. (p. 132)

This passage is taken from Part 3, Chapter 30, where Maurice
denied Clive's sustaining and controlling friendship, is forced to
confront his awakening sexual desire for young men. We see
him here alone and in despair after just rejecting the advances
of a business client, a young Frenchman, at his office. This, in
turn, leads to thoughts of his own attempted seduction of Dickie,
the nephew of a family friend. He resolves to keep clear of
temptation in future, but an encounter with an old man in a
train in the next chapter will precipitate a crisis, driving
Maurice, unsuccessfully, to seek a cure for his condition. Clearly,
then, the conflict here is between Maurice's growing desire that
he sees as morally reprehensible, and an equally strong need to
keep hold of his respectability.

There seems a certain complication in the narrator's attitude
here too. At one level Maurice's gathering 'habit' of honesty is
seen by Forster as a moral advance. To give his feelings for
Dickie the 'very primitive name' of lust is seen to be truthful at
least; but this notion of moral development is rather undercut
by the hysterical self-condemnation that follows. To see himself
as a 'stoat' in a frenzy of self-abasement is no more truthful than
calling his feelings for Dickie 'adoration'. In a way, it is equally
sentimental and obfuscating. After all, 'Poor little Dickie' is a
cadet at a military academy well able to look after himself, and
Maurice's picture of the possible consequences of his action is
somewhat alarmist: broken windows, injury, scandal, a victim
'yelling like a maniac' – and the police. Not that we should ever
forget that Maurice is technically a potential criminal and, in the
eyes of Edwardian society, eventually becomes one. To what
extent, in 1913–14, Forster also thought of himself as one is, of
course, an open question, but we can't be sure that a distancing
irony is operating here. It might be that Maurice's self-disgust is

Forster's also: in which case the controlled distance of art has been exchanged for personal therapy. It's a difficult issue that confronts every careful reader of this text from time to time. Certainly the major emphasis of the second paragraph is class betrayal and class guilt. Forster captures Maurice's self-pity and self-hatred well; his use of clichés – 'advanced to the grindstone' and 'forewarned, and therefore forearmed' – exposes his hero's limited puritan conventionality. 'Lust' is not accepted as a fact of life but rejected by a narrow-minded conformist. It is a sin, not against God, but against the middle classes. 'Settlements' were early youth clubs run by middle-class idealists in the poorer parts of big cities, so Maurice's noble programme of social service is revealed now for what it is – a ploy to be near young working-class men and boys. Maurice wrinkles his nose in disgust at the thought. Then there is the final reproach of the last sentence. Maurice sees himself as a class traitor, self-evidently guilty. We may wish to read the last sentence satirically; if so, it must belong to the intelligent narrator, for irony is not part of Maurice's inflexible mind. Does Forster distance himself or share his hero's sense of guilt, merely stating a fact? I think you'll agree it is not easy to say.

However, whether Forster writes from within this sense of class betrayal or whether he is exposing it, the difficulties of Maurice's emancipation seem formidable. Sex is seen as inherently bad and nothing to do with love: Maurice is a 'gentleman' but he has 'lusts' that he wants to satisfy with 'persons' from the lower classes. He is as far as ever from reconciling the brutality and idealism of his two childhood dreams.

I should like to move on now and look at a passage towards the end of the novel where Maurice has just found a working-class lover.

5 Select a fourth passage for discussion

His chin on his knees, Maurice brooded. A storm of distaste was working up inside him, and he did not know against what to direct it. Whether the ladies spoke, whether Alec blocked Mr Borenius's lobs, whether the villagers clapped or didn't clap, he felt unspeakably oppressed: he had swallowed an unknown drug: he had disturbed his life to its foundations, and couldn't tell what would crumble.

When he went out to bat, it was a new over, so that Alec received first ball. His style changed. Abandoning caution, he swiped the ball into the fern. Lifting his eyes, he met Maurice's and smiled. Lost ball. Next time he hit a boundary. He was untrained, but had the cricketing build, and the game took on some semblance of reality. Maurice played up too. His mind had cleared, and he felt that they were against the whole world, that not only Mr Borenius and the field but the audience in the shed and all England were closing round the wickets. They played for the sake of each other and of their fragile relationship – if one fell the other would follow. They intended no harm to the world, but so long as it attacked they must punish, they must stand wary, then hit with full strength, they must show that when two are gathered together majorities shall not triumph. And as the game proceeded it connected with the night, and interpreted it. Clive ended it easily enough. When he came to the ground they were no longer the leading force; people turned their heads, the game languished, and ceased. Alec resigned. It was only fit and proper that the squire should bat at once. Without looking at Maurice, he receded. He too was in white flannels, and their looseness made him look like a gentleman or anyone else. He stood in front of the shed with dignity, and when Clive had done talking offered his bat, which Clive took as a matter of course: then flung himself down by old Ayres. (pp.176–7)

This passage, taken from Part 4, Chapter 39, describes Maurice's fluctuating emotional state the day after Alec has become his lover. The tension within Maurice is clear at the onset, but this shifts to a sense of conflict between the lovers and the rest of society when they share a partnership during the cricket match. Their elated rediscovery of each other does not survive the return of Clive, however.

At the start, Maurice is set apart from the rest of the action, spectators and players alike, brooding. His feelings for Alec are 'an unknown drug' and are not seen positively; quite the reverse in fact, for Maurice is in that familiar state of self-disgust we noted in the previous passage. The experiences of the previous night have undermined his whole settled way of life and the tone of the language is ominous and minatory. There are images of physical distemper – 'working up inside him', 'unspeakably oppressed', 'swallowed an unknown drug' – and suggestions of seismic upheaval: 'disturb', 'foundations', 'collapse'.

All this changes once Maurice is out at the wicket, partnering Alec in the ritual of the game. He has become a 'partner' in two senses now; he is 'sharing a partnership' in cricket and in metaphorical terms, he and Alec are proclaiming their feelings for each other to an uncomprehending world. 'Abandoning caution', Alec's boundaries are symbolic; they show scorn for society and its rituals. The paradox is that these same rituals lead to 'some semblance of reality' and help clear Maurice's mind. Forster stresses a sense of brave vulnerability: 'they were against the whole world' and 'all England' is 'closing round the wickets'. The language is very beleaguered and embattled: 'attacked', 'punish', 'stand wary', 'hit with full strength', 'majorities shall not triumph'. Through the rituals of the game, Maurice and Alec are 'connected' and so able to interpret their passionate feelings for each other, a classless passion that Forster celebrates with Biblical sonority: 'when two are gathered together majorities shall not triumph'.

But the victory is only temporary: Clive's return symbolises the forces of convention and the power of class hierarchy. The lovers' joy in each other evaporates for 'the squire should bat at once'. Alec must give way to a gentleman, even though he has natural dignity and 'looks like a gentleman' in the anonymity of white flannels; he has to return to his side of the class boundary and sit with the other servants.

Cricket is a powerful metaphor for the workings of English society where an apparent idyllic celebration of unity and social ritual hides real conflict and discontent; the power of the class system is aptly demonstrated by Clive's reception and the fact that Alec feels that he must give way, even though he is doing well. The game has been put to such symbolic purposes by other writers besides Forster. He, however, gives it an additional twist by adding the homosexual dimension.

He shows us that Maurice and Alec's feelings can only be declared metaphorically in a freakish accident that allows them to interpret social conventions in ways that express their own private feelings. Theirs is a forbidden relationship – two 'against the world' – and the world is a formidable enemy to take on, despite the brave talk. Is it possible to transcend class and conventional morality in more normal situations than the one depicted here? Can Mr Borenius's 'lobs' be so lightly treated elsewhere, away from the cricket pitch? Forster may wish fervently that they can, but such a hope remains only a yearned for possibility. I chose this passage because it is the only place in the novel where Maurice is seen to be standing his ground emotionally: 'They played for the sake of each other and of their fragile relationship.' Here, and only here, Forster is prepared to give us a vision of a minority showing solidarity and forcing society to change, rather than retreating in isolated self-disgust. Forster is not able to sustain this position any more than his hero can or envisage any kind of political solution to his problems. Society is seen as dull, inert and conformist, all the finer feelings and possibilities lie outside, but as soon as it asserts its power in the arrival of Clive then these finer feelings are exposed as vulnerable, doomed to defeat.

I feel that this passage exposes the central weakness of Forster's position in this novel. Society can never be changed. Personal happiness is a private magic that can only exist in the spaces that society allows through its ignorance. This belief will give any novelist some complicated problems to solve, because much of the interest in novels is in the interaction between the characters and their society. It goes some way to explain why, as I said at the beginning of the chapter, the fictional texture of this novel is so sketchy and thin. Apart from Maurice himself we don't get to know any character very well, and then we only know him through his sexual problems. Society only exists for Maurice, and so for the reader, as a vague menacing presence.

I think I've got as much as I can from this passage so I'm going to move on to my final step in the basic analysis of any novel. After examining three or four passages, it's always best to finish by asking yourself:

6   *Have I achieved a sufficiently complex sense of the fiction?*

Because *Maurice* is focused so exclusively on one character, and one aspect of one character, I feel I've got a better grasp on the book than I would normally expect to have at this stage. However, I should like to have at least one perspective on Maurice from outside his own consciousness. Also, I said earlier in this chapter that novels were rather like puzzles and I should like to see how Forster solves, or attempts to solve, the problems that he has set himself in this fiction. What sort of future does he envisage for his hero? Can Maurice unite the brutal and ideal in his nature and find his perfect friend? In order to attempt an answer to these questions and shift the perspective away from Maurice himself, I've decided to look more closely at the very end of the novel.

He must rescue his old friend. A feeling of heroism stole over him; and he began to wonder how Scudder could be silenced and whether he would prove extortionate. It was too late to discuss ways and means now, so he invited Maurice to dine with him the following week in his club up in town.

A laugh answered. He had always liked his friend's laugh, and at such a moment the soft rumble of it reassured him: it suggested happiness and security. 'That's right,' he said, and went so far as to stretch his hand into a bush of laurels. 'That's better than making me a long set speech, which convinces neither yourself nor me.' His last words were 'Next Wednesday, say at 7.45. Dinner-jacket's enough, as you know.'

They were his last words, because Maurice had disappeared thereabouts, leaving no trace of his presence except a little pile of the petals of the evening primrose, which mourned from the ground like an expiring fire. To the end of his life Clive was not sure of the exact moment of departure, and with the approach of old age he grew uncertain whether the moment had yet occurred. The Blue Room would glimmer, ferns undulate. Out of some eternal Cambridge his friend began beckoning to him, clothed in the sun, and shaking out the scents and sounds of the May Term.

But at the time he was merely offended at a discourtesy, and compared it with similar lapses in the past. He did not realize that this was the end, without twilight or compromise, that he should never cross Maurice's track again, nor speak to those who had seen him. He waited for a little in the alley, then returned to the house, to correct his proofs and to devise some method of concealing the truth from Anne. (pp. 214–15)

This is Maurice's farewell to Clive seen from Clive's point of view. The conflict is in the irreparable parting of two people who had once been close. Maurice is leaving for a life in the 'greenwood' with his lover; Clive must return to his wife, his duties, his conventional life.

What strikes me immediately about the passage is that in Clive's eyes, and maybe in the writer's and reader's too, Maurice is already a mythical presence, hardly a person at all. He is a laugh from the darkness. It is significant that the parting takes place outside the house in the deserted shrubbery, away from the society that Maurice finds so suffocating and denying of his real self. Clive's thoughts are all of 'rescue' and restoring the social surface of things. He attempts to claim his friend back for respectability but can only stretch his hand into a laurel bush. It seems as if the formality of his invitation is being addressed to a nature spirit for whom a dinner jacket is ludicrously inappropriate. The only evidence of Maurice's presence after his mysterious departure is magical and poetic, a lyrical tribute to dying love: the primrose petals that mourn from the ground 'like an expiring fire.' The rest of the third paragraph takes up this elegiac, dying fall. The writing celebrates a private poetry of dimly remembered intimate moments, memories of Maurice's first visit, and a Cambridge that's now 'eternal' – a privileged space where Maurice, now quite transformed into a spring deity 'clothed in the sun', calls an aged Clive back to some nostalgic eternal youth.

Is this a happy ending? Forster thought so because he desperately wanted one, but the evidence suggests otherwise. As some of Forster's friends thought at the time, it is difficult to envisage a future for the lovers as outlaws in the 'greenwood' outside society. It seems an evasion of the issues that the text proposes to confront. The 'real' Maurice is a bourgeois stockbroker, as appalled as Clive is by his sexual 'fall' with a gamekeeper. The truth is that Maurice never really ceases to see his sexuality as a crippling disability, acceptable only when chaste and redeemed by sentimental poetry. The ending of the novel suggests that Forster feels the same. In these closing paragraphs he smooths away difficulties and contradictions by 'mythologising' Maurice and allowing him to slip away into the woods. By shifting attention to Clive, Forster is able to banish Maurice's feelings of class betrayal and self-loathing. For Maurice's relationship with Alec, lightly sketched as it is, is a descent into hell as well as an ecstatic release – feared as well as desired. This fundamental tension, expressed in the childhood dreams, remains unresolved. There is a refusal on Forster's part to explore the politics of gender and homosexual desire, and relate them to the wider politics of society and class. Clive's social order at Penge remains; it may be decadent, insincere, but it is secure and intact.

Compared with the real constraints, problems and negotiations of Clive's marriage to Anne, Maurice's homosexual romance, dressed up as it is, begins to look rather weightless and insubstantial, a piece of special pleading. Part of the problem here is the power of conventional literary conventions. Forster has to finish his book somehow, and, though heterosexual marriage is seen as flawed and hypocritical, it still acts as a closing device. Even though Forster is writing a private book for himself he is still implicated in the society he wishes to reject. Part of him – perhaps the most important part – remains behind with Clive, yearning for a retrospectively idealised past but committed to a life of compromise and pretence because no other way of life seems realistically possible.

Forster was a complex personality, self-divided and ambiguous towards his society. An examination of *Maurice* goes someway to explain the reasons why. This text represents a particularly crude and direct attempt to reconcile public with private morality. Such an attempt can only be viewed as blatant wish-fulfilment. It is a 'transparent' fiction because it is such a private one. Justifying *Maurice* in a letter to a friend, Forster wrote: 'I was trying to connect up and use all the fragments I was born with.' I've said that texts are puzzles. Forster was only able to solve this puzzle through a theatrical sleight of hand. The ideal and the brutal, the sexual and the emotional, remain divided in Maurice to the end.

Forster is not a 'homosexual writer' in that homosexuality is not the theme of the books that made him famous. But the intimate concerns that are revealed in *Maurice* inform his more considered, public work. I think that we shall find a quest for integration and wholeness at the heart of every novel; Forster's unhappiness, and his ambiguous feelings towards the society that caused it, may be concealed, conventionalised, coded and overlaid by other social, philosophical and moral concerns but, paradoxically, these wider issues are enriched because complicated and deepened by Forster's private pain.

3

The First Italian Novel: *Where Angels Fear to Tread* (1905)

I Constructing an overall analysis

Although the first to be published, *Where Angels Fear to Tread* was not the first novel Forster attempted. This may help explain the confident sophistication of this early work which appeared when Forster was only twenty-six. An account of the plot will show how far removed it is from the comparatively simple narrative of *Maurice*.

1 *After reading the novel, think about the story and what kind of pattern you can see in the text*

Philip Herriton, a young barrister, lives with his mother and sister Harriet near London in respectable, suburban Sawston. The novel opens with the departure of Philip's widowed sister-in-law, Lilia, for a year's travel in Italy, leaving her daughter Irma behind. Lilia is a rather vulgar, silly woman and a social embarrassment to the Herriton family. She has been sent abroad to 'improve' herself in the sober company of Caroline Abbott, a local spinster, who is to act as chaperone although much younger.

But these well-made plans lead to disaster. Evidently encouraged by Caroline, Lilia becomes involved with Gino Carella, a local youth in the small Tuscan town of Monteriano. Philip is dispatched to avert the match by his mother but arrives too late. They are married. The marriage is not a success. Lilia becomes increasingly isolated and lonely in a strange culture she cannot adjust to, and finally dies giving birth to Gino's son.

Affairs in Sawston return to normal and the Herritons concentrate their efforts on bringing up Lilia's daughter. However, domestic tranquillity is rudely dashed when Irma learns of the existence of her Italian half-brother. The Herritons are inclined to ignore his existence but Caroline, overcome with guilt, forces their hand by insisting the child be rescued and brought up in England.

A second rescue party ensues but this only leads to further muddle and eventual tragedy. Caroline sees that Gino loves his son and changes her mind but Harriet, inflexible and determined, kidnaps him, and the baby is subsequently killed in a carriage accident. Philip, who has been ineffectual throughout, returns to tell Gino the news. Crazed with grief, Gino tortures him and is only prevented from killing him by the timely arrival of Caroline.

The novel ends with Caroline and Philip returning to Sawston. By now Philip is in love with Caroline but she, thinking him detached from any strong emotion, confesses her love for Gino. Both have been strongly affected by their experiences but feel they have no alternative other than to return to the constraints and conventions of respectable English society.

After undertaking this first step, I think it is clear that Philip is at the centre of this novel and its subject is his moral education and that, unlike *Maurice*, the novel's plot and narrative organisation extend further and deal with more than just the struggles of one young man to grow up. The title is taken from a famous line from Alexander Pope's poem 'An Essay on Criticism' – 'For Fools rush in where Angels fear to tread' – and this implies a general concern with rashness and impetuosity in the face of new or unfamiliar experiences. Actually Forster was rather unsure of this title, chosen by a friend; his own was simply 'Monteriano' but this was disliked by his publisher. The rejected title highlights another concern of the book, namely an interest in Italian life and culture. Certainly Monteriano provides a challenge to the respectable, middle-class conformity of Sawston and, if I consider my synopsis, I can see that the novel is built around a conflict between these two markedly different ways of life. Philip may have a central role in this conflict but it extends beyond him: his problems are placed in a wider social and cultural context.

I can see, too, that the structure of the novel is neatly symmetrical and is based on the idea of travel. The book begins and ends with a railway journey and falls carefully into two halves. The first four chapters concern Lilia's journey to Italy, Philip's attempt to save her from Gino, and her sad end. It would seem that Lilia is a 'fool' who has rushed into an experience that she cannot handle, but Caroline and Philip are also made to look foolish and return to England chastened and disillusioned. This is the first cycle of the narrative. Chapter 5 is an interlude and, like Chapter 1, is based in Sawston. Also like Chapter 1, it ends in uproar and upheaval as Mrs Herriton dispatches Philip to Italy once again, this time with Harriet as moral support. The second half of the novel is really a repetition yet variation of the first: again the English travellers get tangled up in events they can't understand or control, and again the outcome is disaster and death, though this time the lives and understanding of Philip and Caroline are significantly enlarged.

Philip's part in all this travelling to and fro is obviously central; though Caroline is crucial to the plot and also experiences the transforming and disturbing power of Italy, she is a rather shadowy and enigmatic figure; it is through Philip that we experience the tension between the two cultures most acutely.

Now we've sorted this out, the best way forward is to move on to our second step and begin to examine Philip more closely. I think a good understanding of his development will provide us with the basis for a sound analysis of the novel as a whole.

2   Select a short passage featuring one of the main characters and try to build upon the ideas you have established so far

I've chosen a passage in the middle of the opening chapter where Philip and his mother are discussing Lilia after her departure for Italy (page references to the novel relate to the Penguin edition, 1988).

> Mrs Herriton replied, 'When a man is neither well-bred, nor well-connected, nor handsome, nor clever, nor rich, even Lilia may discard him in time.'

'No. I believe she would take any one. Right up to the last, when her boxes were packed, she was "playing" the chinless curate. Both the curates are chinless, but hers had the dampest hands. I came on them in the Park. They were speaking of the Pentateuch.'

'My dear boy! If possible, she has got worse and worse. It was your idea of Italian travel that saved us!'

Philip brightened at the little compliment. 'The odd part is that she was quite eager – and always asking me for information; and of course I was very glad to give it. I admit she is a Philistine, appallingly ignorant, and her taste in art is false. Still, to have any taste at all is something. And I do believe that Italy really purifies and ennobles all who visit her. She is the school as well as the playground of the world. It is really to Lilia's credit that she wants to go there.'

'She would go anywhere,' said his mother, who had heard enough of the praises of Italy. 'I and Caroline Abbott had the greatest difficulty in dissuading her from the Riviera.'

'No, mother; no. She was really keen on Italy. This travel is quite a crisis for her.' He found the situation full of whimsical romance: there was something half-attractive, half-repellent in the thought of this vulgar woman journeying to places he loved and revered. Why should she not be transfigured? The same had happened to the Goths.

Mrs Herriton did not believe in romance, nor in transfiguration, nor in parallels from history, nor in anything else that may disturb domestic life. She adroitly changed the subject before Philip got excited. (pp. 22–3)

I said in my last chapter that it is best to have a plan when examining passages like this. It's easy to miss things unless you have a structured approach and in this chapter I'm going to show you a way of building up an analysis. As before, I shall look for some conflict or tension in each passage, but this time I'm going to let you into my method and demonstrate how you can go about this, stage by stage. These are the steps I shall follow:

(a) *Make a short statement of what the passage is about*
(b) *Search for an opposition or tension within the passage*
(c) *Analyse the details of the passage, relating them to the opposition already noted*

(d) *Try to say how the passage relates to the novel as a whole*
(e) *Search for anything distinctive about the passage, particularly in the area of style, which you have not already noted*

I'm now going to make points under each of these headings in turn. It's surprising how quickly you can accumulate material in this way.

(a) *Make a short statement of what the passage is about*

Philip and his mother are discussing Lilia's character and her motives for choosing Italy for her travels.

(b) *Search for an opposition or tension within the passage*

Clearly there is some disagreement between the two: Philip thinks that Lilia wishes to reform and is seeking culture and enlightenment; his mother thinks she is merely after pleasure and excitement. More subtly, I think we can see an additional tension in Philip's character presented here. On the one hand he comes over as mocking and cynically self-superior; on the other, he has a vein of rather naïve idealism. His character doesn't seem to be of a piece – and this is interesting.

(c) *Analyse the details of the passage, relating them to the opposition already noted*

The passage opens with Mrs Herriton's scornful dismissal of Lilia. It's an elegantly controlled sentence, dominated by negatives and with a sting at the end. There is heavy irony in the use of 'even', 'may' and 'in time'. The implication is, of course, that Lilia has no judgement at all, and wouldn't discard any man who showed an interest in her.

Though, at this point, Philip appears to disagree with his mother, he is in fact agreeing with her and amusing himself at Lilia's expense. He mocks her timid suitor, the chinless curate, and the unlikelihood of Lilia being interested in theological discussions. He enjoys the opportunity of satirising Lilia as a flirt, and the dull earnestness of respectable religion. This allows him to cut a dash and appear unconventional, but in fact he is playing his mother's game. He is her foil and needs her good opinion; this becomes apparent when he shows pleasure at her compliment.

However, as the conversation develops, significant differences do begin to emerge: Philip becomes enthusiastic despite his rather pompous sense of his own superiority; his pleasure in Italy, though bookish and idealistic, mitigates his complacent dismissal of Lilia as an appalling Philistine, ignorant about art. Again his mother brings things down to earth. She insists that Lilia is not motivated by noble ideals – 'She would go anywhere' – but in having a good time. I think we feel that she may well be right, but we don't like her any the better for it, or her need to contain Philip by changing the subject. It is significant, I feel, that apart from 'the little compliment', her conversation and thoughts are entirely negative; this is not true of Philip: 'And I do believe that Italy really purifies and ennobles . . . It is really to Lilia's credit . . . She was really keen on Italy . . . quite a crisis for her . . . journeying to places he loved and revered'. Such enthusiasm has the effect of enlisting us on his side of the argument.

(d) *Try to say how the passage relates to the novel as a whole*

Of course, it's too early to say much under this heading except that the passage shows Mrs Herriton's dominant nature, her artful diplomacy, and her need to reduce everything to the even temper of domestic order. As we've noted, her conversation is dominated by negatives and dismissals. However priggish and self-satisfied Philip is, he does have the capacity for a wider, more generous view of life. He obviously feels that there should be more to life than conforming to his mother's norms of social respectability and Italy is the focus for this discontent. She, aware of this, seems determined to head off his rebellion by a subtle combination of flattery and patronising parental control: 'She adroitly changed the subject before Philip got excited.'

(e) *Search for anything distinctive about the passage, particularly in the area of style, which you have not already noted*

The passage begins with dialogue but this gives way to an omniscient narrator and, stylistically, this is a very important feature in any Forster novel. The narrator knows what is going on in the minds of both speakers. At some points this narrator is external – Philip 'brightened' at his mother's compliment – but at other times he will give us the character's thoughts, even to the extent of becoming at one with both Philip and his mother in places, while maintaining an ironic distance and overview of the whole action. An example of what I mean would be: 'Why should she not be transfigured? The same had happened to the Goths'. This trick of expressing first person thought in third person narrative, in effect 'miming' the character, is called 'free indirect speech' and can be used for ironic effect. This is because the character's thoughts are put into a broader, more critical perspective.

It's through the mediation of the narrator in this way that we enjoy Philip's farcical romanticism as he contemplates Lilia's possible transfiguration and compares her to the Goths. He is attempting to construct a dramatic narrative out of Lilia's journey and we know enough already to feel this is absurdly removed from the reality of the situation. On the other hand, Mrs Herriton's dismissal of Italy is comic too; it is seen to be prejudiced and narrowly conventional. To sum up, then, the narrative presence here or, to put it another way, Forster's narrative 'persona', is wiser and more comprehensive than either of the two participants. Philip and his mother judge Lilia but they, in their turn, are judged by the narrator and his all-persuasive ironic tone. This authorial presence is asserting its control, determining our attitude to both mother and son, and finally, I feel, judges Mrs Herriton rather more severely than Philip. Her practical level-headedness is not seen as a virtue, as it might be, say, in a Jane Austen novel (a novelist to whom Forster is often compared), but part of a snobbish, negative and limited view of life.

I'm now going on to look at another passage in the next chapter when Philip travels to Italy in an attempt to stop Lilia's marriage.

3 Select a second passage for discussion

'Gentlemen sometimes judge hardly. But I feel that you, and at all events your mother – so really so good in every sense, so really unworldly – after all, love – marriages are made in heaven.'

'Yes, Miss Abbott, I know. But I am anxious to hear heaven's choice. You arouse my curiosity. Is my sister-in-law to marry an angel?'

'Mr Herriton, don't – please, Mr Herriton – a dentist. His father's a dentist.'

Philip gave a cry of personal disgust and pain. He shuddered all over, and edged away from his companion. A dentist! A dentist at Monteriano. A dentist in fairy land! False teeth and laughing gas and the tilting chair at a place which knew the Etruscan League, and the Pax Romana, and Alaric himself, and the Countess Matilda, and the Middle Ages, all fighting and holiness, and the Renaissance, all fighting and beauty! He thought of Lilia no longer. He was anxious for himself: he feared that Romance might die.

Romance only dies with life. No pair of pincers will ever pull it out of us. But there is a spurious sentiment which cannot resist the unexpected and the incongruous and the grotesque. A touch will loosen it, and the sooner it goes from us the better. It was going from Philip now, and therefore he gave the cry of pain. (pp. 37–8)

(a) *Make a short statement of what the passage is about*

Philip learns of Gino's background from Caroline Abbott on his way from the station to Monteriano.

(b) *Search for an opposition or tension within the passage*

As Caroline has condoned Lilia's relationship, she is clearly anxious and embarrassed. There is a tension in her reluctance to tell the truth and Philip's impatience to learn it.

(c) *Analyse the details of the passage, relating them to the opposition already noted*

There is a good deal of social comedy in the first part of this passage. We've seen enough of Mrs Herriton by now to know just how worldly she is; as far as the Herritons are concerned, marriages are most definitely made on earth. Caroline's tentative approach is well captured by the halting *non sequiturs* and incomplete sentences. We can enjoy Philip's heavy irony as he chooses to take the cliché 'marriages are made in heaven' literally. The pompous formality of his speech is in comic contrast to Caroline's breathless embarrassment.

The tone of the passage and the mode of address changes after Philip learns the truth. There is still comedy in Philip's alarm and despair but it is interior, private to him, and presented in a mixture of critical commentary and authorial sympathy. Philip's horror speaks volumes about Edwardian class snobbery and the relatively low status of dentists at the time, but, of course, there's more to it than this. There's been a rude insertion of the real world into Philip's academic and exclusively aesthetic fantasy of Italy and Italian life. I don't think it is necessary to know who or what the Etruscan League, the Pax Romana, Alaric and the Countess Matilda are, to get the point. Philip's Italy is 'fairy land'. His sheltered life has given him no insight into the painful complexities behind the academic books and the beautiful pictures. His Italy belongs all too exclusively to the world of art and scholarship. The give-away, I think, is in the phrasing of 'the Middle Ages, all fighting and holiness, and the Renaissance, all fighting and beauty!' He has no insight into the brutality and the human cost behind the glories and achievements of Italy's past. Gino's existence forces him to confront an actual contemporary Italy with a real social existence, not an ideal that he can use to escape from Sawston and life with his mother.

In the last paragraph there is a further move away from Philip's thoughts to direct authorial commentary. The narrator judges Philip's 'spurious sentiment' that can only accept life on its own exclusive terms, taking up the metaphor of dentistry and using it to good effect; such feelings are like a rotten tooth and Philip is well rid of them.

(d) *Try to show how the passage relates to the novel as a whole*

Clearly this is the beginning, the first stage, of Philip's moral education. This is his first confrontation with the 'real' Italy and not the exclusive one of the Baedeker guide books. Painful but necessary, it leads to disillusionment, but the narrator implies that it will not last: 'Romance only dies with life'.

(e) *Search for anything distinctive about the passage, particularly in the area of style, which you have not already noted*

I think it's worth noting again how skilfully Forster manipulates his narrative persona, working at several levels. First there is the objective presentation of the social comedy where we stand apart and enjoy the discomfiture of both parties, then the interior expression of Philip's alarm and despair presented somewhat ironically in the detached third person, and, finally, the general comments made with a more comprehensive understanding of the whole situation. As in the first passage, the narrator guides our responses. Philip is satirical at Caroline Abbott's expense and then, in his turn, is satirised without ever quite losing our sympathy. This is a considerable achievement, for Forster does not conceal Philip's failings at this stage, his selfishness, his snobbishness, or his effete fastidiousness.

4 Select a third passage for discussion

Now I'm going to take a passage much further into the book to get some sense of Philip's development.

'You are wonderful!' he said gravely.

'Oh, you appreciate me!' she burst out again. 'I wish you didn't. You appreciate us all – see good in all of us. And all the time you are dead – dead – dead. Look, why aren't you angry?' She came up to him, and then her mood suddenly changed, and she took hold of both his hands. 'You are so splendid, Mr Herriton, that I can't bear to see you wasted. I can't bear – she has not been good to you – your mother.'

'Miss Abbott, don't worry over me. Some people are born not to do things. I'm one of them; I never did anything at school or at the Bar. I came out to stop Lilia's marriage, and it was too late. I came out intending to get the baby, and I shall return an "honourable failure". I never expect anything to happen now, and so I am never disappointed. You would be surprised to know what my great events are. Going to the theatre yesterday, talking to you now – I don't suppose I shall ever meet anything greater. I seem fated to pass through the world without colliding with it or moving it – and I'm sure I can't tell you whether the fate's good or evil. I don't die – I don't fall in love. And if other people die or fall in love they always do it when I'm just not there. You are quite right; life to me is just a spectacle, which – thank God, and thank Italy, and thank you – is now more beautiful and heartening than it has ever been before.'

She said solemnly, 'I wish something would happen to you, my dear friend; I wish something would happen to you.'

'But why?' he asked, smiling. 'Prove to me why I don't do as I am.'

She also smiled, very gravely. She could not prove it. No argument existed. Their discourse, splendid as it had been, resulted in nothing, and their respective opinions and policies were exactly the same when they left the church as when they had entered it. (pp. 134–5)

(a) *Make a short statement of what the passage is about*

This passage is taken from Chapter 8. It is part of a conversation that takes place between Caroline Abbott and Philip in the church of Santa Deodata after they have both seen Gino and the baby.

(b) *Search for an opposition or tension within the passage*

Caroline is attempting to make Philip see the need to be decisive about what is best for the baby's future and make a clear moral choice. All that Philip can do is declare his moral bankruptcy. There is an obvious conflict between her moral passion, her exasperation, and his resigned passivity.

(c) *Analyse the details of the passage, relating them to the opposition already noted*

The first thing to strike me is Caroline's anger. There is passion here that bursts through the social decorum that's been so evident in the earlier passages. In her candid frankness – 'you are dead – dead – dead' – and her sudden switch to tender concern – 'You are so splendid, Mr Herriton, that I can't bear to see you wasted' – Caroline is acting the role of the true friend. Her judgement of Mrs Herriton is, we feel sure, the right one, so we trust her.

Philip's long speech shows a degree of insight and sombre self-assessment he has not shown before. It's a depressing admission 'of moral defeat that is partially redeemed by its honesty. Unlike those speeches and thoughts of his in the earlier passages which were mocking or self-regarding, this has the unmistakable accents of sincerity – and this saves it from being merely indulgent self-pity. It's clear that under the cynical pose Philip doesn't think much of himself. The simple, declarative, first person sentences are dominated by negatives: 'don't worry ... born not to do things ... I never did anything ... too late ... "honourable failure", ... I never expect ... I am never disappointed ... I don't suppose ... I can't tell you ... I don't die – I don't fall in love ... when I'm just not there'.

This makes the 'great events', the theatre trip, the present conversation, even more pitiable in their limitation, because we feel that Philip is speaking the truth. His emotional life is desperately impoverished. There is, too, a rather pathetic gratitude in Philip's reaching out for another human being that belies that he is willingly one of life's spectators. Italy is now a real place, not a cultural museum, and inhabited by real people: 'thank God, and thank Italy, and thank you.'

(d) *Try to say how the passage relates to the novel as a whole*

Much has happened in the narrative since the last passage we examined, not least being a dramatic shift in the relationship between Caroline and Philip. Philip has experienced a humiliating defeat over Lilia's marriage and clearly expects another one over the baby. Yet he has learnt much about himself and he has gained a friend. Neither Philip nor Caroline could have been drawn so close or spoken with such honesty in stuffy, reserved Sawston. Italy, despite all the muddle, confusion and potential for betrayal, is the place for warmth and truth-telling in personal relationships. It heightens emotional affinities and makes for strange alliances between kindred spirits. Lilia's infatuation and Caroline's uncharacteristic behaviour condoning it, become increasingly explicable as the book progresses. Both Philip and Caroline have been changed by their Italian experiences. Like Lilia, they have been 'transfigured', though not in ways Mrs Herriton or the earlier Philip could have anticipated or understood. 'Romance' has not died as Philip had feared, but there is a notable absence here of false romance, or what the narrator in the previous passage called 'spurious sentiment'.

(e) *Search for anything distinctive about the passage, particularly in the area of style, which you have not already noted*

The writing is more impassioned, direct and emotional, and there is an absence of the social comedy that was a feature of the earlier passages. Because irony appears to be absent, one might be tempted to feel that there is a retreat from authorial control at this elevated moment of truth-telling, but this would not be true. The discussion ends with the narrator reminding us, with great sadness, of the weakness and limitations of words, the difficulty of communication, amid the troubling complexity of life: 'Their discourse, splendid as it had been, resulted in nothing . . .'

5 Select a fourth passage for discussion

Caroline wishes that 'something would happen' to Philip and, finally, something does. He stands by, ineffectually, while the baby dies and then forces himself to confront his part in the responsibility for the tragedy by being the one to tell Gino. The consequences are terrible and form the climax of Philip's moral education. I shall take a passage from the end of the scene which takes place in Chapter 9.

> Gino spoke for the first time. 'Put the milk on the table,' he said. 'It will not be wanted in the other room.' The peril was over at last. A great sob shook the whole body, another followed, and then he gave a piercing cry of woe, and stumbled towards Miss Abbott like a child and clung to her.
>
> All through the day Miss Abbott had seemed to Philip like a goddess, and more than ever did she seem so now. Many people look younger and more intimate during great emotion. But some there are who look older, and remote, and he could not think there was little difference in years, and none in composition, between her and the man whose head was laid upon her breast. Her eyes were open, full of infinite pity and full of majesty, as if they discerned the boundaries of sorrow, and saw unimaginable tracts beyond. Such eyes he had seen in

great pictures but never in a mortal. Her hands were folded
round the sufferer, stroking him lightly, for even a goddess
can do no more than that. And it seemed fitting, too, that she
should bend her head and touch his forehead with her lips.

Philip looked away, as he sometimes looked away from the
great pictures where visible forms suddenly become inadequate for the things they have shown to us. He was happy; he
was assured that there was greatness in the world. There came
to him an earnest desire to be good through the example of
this good woman. He would try henceforward to be worthy of
the things she had revealed. Quietly, without hysterical
prayers or banging of drums, he underwent conversion. He
was saved.

'That milk,' said she, 'need not be wasted. Take it, Signor
Carella, and persuade Mr Herriton to drink.' (pp. 151–2)

(a) *Make a short statement of what the passage is about*

Caroline Abbott has arrived just in time to stop Gino murdering
Philip, and to comfort him. Philip, looking on in his own
weakened and exhausted state, experiences some kind of ultimate revelation into the nature of human goodness and human
possibility.

(b) *Search for an opposition or tension within the passage*

This is quite difficult because, after the terrible cruelty and
violence of Gino's torture, all Forster's efforts in this passage are
exerted towards creating a moment of reconciliation, expressed
in visionary terms. I think the tension must be between Gino and
Caroline, emotionally bonded by the need to give and receive
comfort, and Philip who, witnessing this, is still excluded, still
one of life's spectators. Put in a slightly different way, I see a
tension here between the raw, painful experiences of life and
the efforts of Philip (and the narrator) to express and make
sense of them in terms of the more formal organisations of art.

(c) *Analyse the details of the passage, relating them to the opposition
     already noted*

The focus in the first part of the passage is on Gino's grief and
Caroline's comfort. After the rawness of the 'piercing cry', the

childlike stumbling and clinging, the scene is deliberately reduced to a static tableau; it becomes a 'composition' rather like a
painting. Caroline is ageless, 'remote'. She is deified as 'a
goddess', her eyes 'full of majesty' and 'full of infinite pity' as she
holds Gino in her arms. Philip has seen such an expression and
such a scene only in 'great pictures'. I don't think there is much
doubt what pictures he has in mind. What Forster has given us
here is a reworking of a great religious subject for classical
painting, the crucified body of Jesus in the arms of the Virgin
Mary, or what art historians call the *pietà*. For Philip, Caroline
transcends her own humanity by seeming to discern 'the boundaries of sorrow' and the 'unimaginable tracts beyond'. There is a
paradox in that, as a 'goddess', she can only give the human
comfort of stroking and kissing; in other words, the most divine
attribute is to show human care. Spirituality and vision are
expressed in a human not a supernatural context. This idea is
clearly expressed in the milk that features at the beginning and
at the end of the passage. Though earthy and mundane in itself,
it is obviously intended to be sacramental and symbolises the
need for forgiveness and healing brotherhood.

The second half of the passage shifts the attention to Philip
and his response to his vision. This is difficult to analyse but the
suggestion is, I think, that he has made some kind of integration
of the moral and the aesthetic in his character and so is
redeemed from social triviality. By having his vision of 'the
greatness in the world', Philip achieves a breakthrough into a
different order of reality; he undergoes a sudden conversion or,
in the language of evangelical piety that Forster uses here, he is
'saved', but without any showy external trappings like 'hysterical
prayers' or the 'banging of drums'. It seems as if Philip achieves
his conversion through his aesthetic training and sensibility but
has to be humbled, to be reminded that 'great pictures' are not
adequate in themselves but can only show the way to higher
realities. By realising this, he is enabled to move beyond a love of
culture appreciated for its own sake and grasp a grander vision
of human life.

(d) *Try to say how the passage relates to the novel as a whole*

This passage is the climax in a sequence of revelations for Philip
during the fateful last day in Monteriano before the 'rescue

party' are due to leave, with or without the baby, for home. They often seem to contain moral messages for Philip while he prefers to see beautiful pictures. Earlier in the day, Caroline visits Gino and understands that he loves his child. She helps him wash the baby and this is seen by Philip on his arrival as a charming aesthetic tableau from Renaissance painting: 'the Virgin and Child, with Donor' (p. 126). He doesn't understand the significance of his association because, unlike Caroline, he always seeks to view life through art. Later, when he has his interview with Caroline in the church of Santa Deodata, they are standing under a fresco of the saint, canonised for her inactivity. It is clear that Forster intends us to see a connection between the saint and Philip's own passivity, a connection that Philip cannot recognise. Only here, after the baby's death, can Philip use art to a greater end, or can he? The narrator assures us that he is 'saved', but there is nothing in subsequent events to suggest any great change of life. He seems content to stay one of life's spectators to the end. Clearly there is a problem here that needs further attention.

(e) *Search for anything distinctive about the passage, particularly in the area of style, which you have not already noted*

The distancing authorial irony that I've noted as such a feature of Forster's style in earlier passages does not seem to be operating here. Because of this, the distinction between the narrator and Philip has been lost – or at least blurred; the narrator seems implicated in Philip's aesthetic way of seeing; he shares Philip's view of Gino and Caroline as a picture. The tone is quite different, too; there's a seriousness and an elevated prophetic voice that is formal and solemn. We can see this in the formality of phrasing, the inversions and unusual word order: 'But some there are ... Such eyes he had seen ... There came to him an earnest desire ... He would try henceforward to be worthy'. Forster also gets this solemnity through the use of repetition: 'full of infinite pity and full of majesty'; 'Philip looked away, as he sometimes looked away'; 'to be good through example of this good woman'. Because Forster is writing in an altogether different mode, more visionary and simply assertive, he seems to be endorsing what, previously, he has been criticising Philip for doing, namely seeing life through the spectacles of art. We cannot be sure that Forster has seen the irony in this fact. There is much we have to take on trust here if we accept that Philip has learnt to live properly.

We have now looked at four passages concerning Philip that trace his development through the book. It is now time to assess the progress we have made in our basic analysis by asking a final question.

6 Have I achieved a sufficiently complex sense of the novel?

Well, by just thinking about four passages in a structured and methodical way, I think we have made significant progress. We know a lot more about Philip. In the first passage he had wondered if Lilia might not be 'transfigured' by her Italian experiences like 'the Goths', but in the fourth passage we have seen him 'transfigured' in a way unimaginable at the beginning of the novel. Through his Italian journeys, a rather callow, supercilious youth discovers his own limitations and learns a great deal more about life. Italy has tested him and found him wanting, but through a necessary disillusionment and finally real suffering, Philip has learnt a more generous capacity for love and understanding. As Philip's development is at the heart of the novel, these are significant gains. I have also learnt something of Philip's relationship with his mother and Caroline Abbott. Enough to see that Mrs Herriton may be the villain of the piece and that Caroline has an important role as confidante and friend. My analysis has shown me some interesting features of Forster's style, too. It's clear that an omniscient narrator is essential to his narrative method, his way of telling the story. This narrator overlooks and overhears the action, sometimes intervening to comment on the action, sometimes entering the consciousness of the characters. It would seem from the evidence so far that this narrator makes Philip a figure of fun at the beginning of the book but draws closer to him, maybe even to the point of identifying with his problems, towards the end.

I've also been able to note some interesting variations in Forster's style. He clearly has a gift for convincing dialogue and for making acute social observations of a satirical kind. However, if he has a playful ironic way when dealing with the social surfaces of life, he seems to write more intensely, even religiously, when writing about serious issues, especially moments of crisis or moral choice. All this information is helpful and represents a substantial gain.

I've also been made aware of things I don't know enough about and need to follow up. I need to know more about the other Sawston visitors to Italy, not just Philip and Caroline, important though they are, but silly Lilia and the awful Harriet. Their experiences are also important – they add dimension and depth to the novel's theme. Philip, Caroline, Lilia, Harriet, they are all 'fools' – but they are not all fools in the same way. Then there is the whole social world of the novel: I could see from my synopsis of the plot that the novel is built around the contrast between two ways of life and I need to explore this further. How does Forster contrast life in Sawston and life in Monteriano? In particular the role of Gino must be crucial.

All the plot and all the emotions of the English characters are centred on him to a greater or less degree. He must be examined more closely. What is it he has to teach these respectable middle-class English tourists? Also, I feel the need to examine Forster's style and narrative techniques rather more carefully; how he seems a writer who gives us a very solid sense of the world at one moment, but then can suddenly shift into a way of writing that is altogether more insubstantial, lyrical and even visionary the next. Finally, there is the end of the novel. Though this is supposed to be an 'education novel' it's not at all clear what it is that Philip has learnt. The ending is curiously muted because Philip and Caroline appear to return home intent on living much as before. It will be worth trying to unravel why Forster gives us an end like this. I could go on and I'm sure you could add your own questions and problems to this list.

In the second half of this chapter I'm going to examine some of these problems and wider interests under the heading of *aspects* of the novel. It's clear that much work is still to be done before I can claim to have a full sense of the novel's complexity but I feel I have made a good start; it's just a question of working out from our basic analysis to these different areas of the text by examining other short passages. Studying a novel for an exam is demanding; a sound basic analysis makes the task more manageable. It is something you can do on your own. It should enable you to get some measure of control over the text, help you to establish your priorities and allow you to follow up your own interests with confidence.

II   Aspects of the novel

I'd like to begin by looking at the end of the first chapter. This chapter is full of social comedy and establishes very quickly and deftly the sort of place that Sawston is. It begins with Lilia's departure for Italy; there's some background and family history, and a sense of the Herriton family routine. All this is suddenly disrupted by the news of Lilia's engagement while Harriet and her mother are sowing some spring vegetables in the garden. Panic and chaos ensue; there's much bad temper and domestic strife but eventually Mrs Herriton regains control of the situation. A battle plan is drawn up and Philip is dispatched for Italy. The chapter ends thus:

> Before Mrs Herriton went to bed she wrote to Mrs Theobald, using plain language about Lilia's conduct, and hinting that it was a question on which every one must take sides. She added, as if it was an afterthought, that Mrs Theobald's letter had arrived that morning.
> Just as she was going upstairs she remembered that she never covered up those peas. It upset her more than anything, and again and again she struck the banisters with vexation. Late as it was, she got a lantern from the toolshed and went down the garden to rake the earth over them. The sparrows had taken every one. But countless fragments of the letter remained, disfiguring the tidy ground. (p. 32)

The first paragraph establishes Mrs Herriton's skill in power politics and the arts of forceful diplomacy. There's a need to put Lilia's mother in her place and assert her dominance and control over the situation. The fact that her daughter-in-law chose to inform her through Mrs Theobald rather than writing herself angers Mrs Herriton most of all because it is seen as a direct challenge to her authority, but she conceals this as an 'afterthought'. Her own wounded pride, which is the true motive for the letter, is concealed in a lot of lofty moralising of a particularly black and white kind: 'it was a question on which every one must take sides'. This bullying and judgmental attitude to morality and the manner in which it is tied up with social prejudices, displayed most clearly by Harriet, is shown by Forster as typically 'Sawstonian': the satirical intention is clear.

But if we move on to the final paragraph we can see that the writing here is stranger and the inference altogether more oblique.

Mrs Theobald's letter had arrived at the climax of the spring planting. The peas, we are told, were left to last because they were 'the greatest fun' (p. 26), but, in her anger at the news, Mrs Herriton tore up her letter, scattered the fragments on the ground, and left for the house leaving the peas sown but still uncovered. Now she remembers her unfinished business and her annoyance seems strangely excessive: 'again and again she struck the banisters with vexation.' Even though it is dark and late she goes out to complete her task, only to find that the sparrows have eaten all the peas but the fragments of the letter remain, 'disfiguring the tidy ground.' What are we to make of the rather mysterious and inconclusive end of this first chapter?

Well, I think it shows us that Forster can write in a very lyrical and poetic way as well as being a shrewd social satirist. He is still criticising Mrs Herriton and exposing her limitations, but in a manner that allows images to speak for themselves and linger in the mind. The peas, the sparrows, the torn fragments of paper and the tidy ground, are simply themselves but they also seem to stand for ideas and notions that extend beyond them; they function as symbols. Once you are alerted to this, reading Forster becomes exciting and demanding in unexpected ways. He seems quite straightforward but this is deceptive; no detail in Forster's novels is casual, nothing is merely by chance. You need to read very carefully. When you do, I think you will see that quite small objects, details, even phrases, keep reappearing in different contexts as you go along, gathering meaning and significance all the time. An example of what I mean is Harriet's infamous inlaid box, 'lent not given' to Lilia in the opening scene. Because of Harriet's anxiety to retrieve it, it reappears several times until it becomes a symbol of Harriet's inhibited insecurity and nagging possessiveness.

The details here don't return as a leitmotif or repeated musical phrase in this way, but they do have a resonance; you need to think about them and construct a meaning for yourself. My own feeling, and it might not be yours, is that the scene exposes Mrs Herriton's need to control nature, a project that is doomed to failure because nature is always liable to break out and frustrate well-laid schemes and plans. Just as Lilia has broken out of Sawston respectability, so the sparrows have spoiled Mrs Herriton's cherished plans for cultivation. Indeed, it is Mrs Herriton's own uncontrollable outbreak of temper that has brought this about. Though she may not choose to acknowledge it, she, too, is subject to natural impulses. The message seems to be that when you work against nature there is waste – the peas get eaten – but also there is disfigurement and destruction – the torn paper litters the tidy ground. Moreover, at least the sparrows benefit from the peas so they serve nature, however unintentionally, but the torn paper fragments seem an image of destruction, seeds of anger that can yield no useful harvest. Because she values social propriety above all else, Mrs Herriton has chosen to deny life and this may have unforeseen consequences.

You may wish to read this paragraph in a different way or change the emphasis that I have given it; the important point is that some interpretation is necessary. Forster's clear intention is to leave the meaning open so that we have to read responsively and draw conclusions for ourselves. Finally, I think it is worthwhile reminding ourselves that Philip is on his way to Italy. The ending of this first chapter strikes a warning note. Frustrations in Sawston may merely be a prefiguration of more serious frustrations in Monteriano.

I'm going to move on now and look at quite a long passage describing Philip's first meeting with Gino in Chapter 2:

> Signor Carella, heartened by the spaghetti and the throat-rasping wine, attempted to talk, and looking politely towards Philip, said, 'England is a great country. The Italians love England and the English.'
>
> Philip, in no mood for international amenities, merely bowed.
>
> 'Italy too,' the other continued a little resentfully, 'is a great country. She has produced many famous men – for example, Garibaldi and Dante. The latter wrote the "Inferno", the "Purgatorio", the "Paradiso". The "Inferno" is the most beautiful.' And with the complacent tone of one who has received a solid education, he quoted the opening lines –
>
>> Nel mezzo del cammin di nostra vita
>> Mi ritrovai per una selva oscura,
>> Che la diritta via era smarrita –

a quotation which was more apt than he supposed.

Lilia glanced at Philip to see whether he noticed that she was marrying no ignoramus. Anxious to exhibit all the good qualities of her betrothed, she abruptly introduced the subject of Pallone, in which, it appeared, he was a proficient player. He suddenly became shy, and developed a conceited grin – the grin of the village yokel whose cricket score is mentioned before a stranger. Philip himself had loved to watch Pallone, that entrancing combination of lawn-tennis and fives. But he did not expect to love it quite so much again.

'Oh, look!' exclaimed Lilia, 'the poor wee fish!'

A starved cat had been worrying them for pieces of the purple quivering beef they were trying to swallow. Signor Carella, with the brutality so common in Italians, had caught her by the paw and flung her away from him. Now she had climbed up to the bowl and was trying to hook out the fish. He got up, drove her off, and finding a large glass stopper by the bowl, entirely plugged up the aperture with it.

'But may not the fish die?' said Miss Abbott. 'They have no air.'

'Fish live on water, not on air,' he replied in a knowing voice, and sat down. Apparently he was at his ease again, for he took to spitting on the floor. (pp. 41–2)

I've chosen to quote a generous portion of this meeting because it allows us to see the extraordinary nimbleness and dexterity of Forster's writing in operation; this passage begins with comedy of manners, ends in broad farce, but has something more serious in between. It is, of course, highly comic, for it shows a clash of cultures with both sides at their worst. Neither Sawston nor Italy come off with much credit here. Philip is pompous, Gino ingratiating and coarse; Lilia attempts, with a proprietorial air, to show Gino off, while Caroline is tense and anxious.

We begin with the comic formality of the 'international amenities': Gino parades his schoolboy learning, which, in the circumstances, is ludicrously inappropriate for one of Philip's education and interest in Italian culture. Of course, the major part of the fun in this whole developing exchange is Gino's behaviour; he simply cannot be contained for long within the constraints of polite conversation. Unlike the English visitors, he has no social graces; this contrasts amusingly with Philip's frosty reserve. Rather like a small boy, Gino is anarchic and unpredictable: brash and complacent, vulgar, brutal and shy by turns. His uninhibited physical nature is shown in the rough way he handles the cat and spits on the floor. His treatment of the fish may reveal his ignorance, but we can still believe that he is a force to be reckoned with.

Referring to his proficiency at Pallone, the narrator compares Gino to a conceited village yokel but, of course, his strength lies in his lack of class in this English sense. Because he is impossible to 'place', it is impossible to put him in his place. Sawston's snobbery and demand for class-conscious 'respectability' prove quite ineffectual here in Monteriano, where the rules of English social behaviour and class hierarchy simply don't apply. Italian life works on a simpler, grander scale; though it may be coarse, it has the effect of making the English look rather drab and foolishly inhibited. Gino's treatment of the 'poor wee fish' is highly amusing, but I can't help feeling the real weight of the satire falls on the English. Again there is that conflict between the need to control nature and the way that nature will keep irrepressibly breaking out that I noted in the first passage. Rather like the bothersome cat, Gino finally doesn't care whether his actions are socially acceptable or not.

The narrator is once again omnisciently in control, entering into Philip's consciousness over the matter of the Pallone so that the bias of the narrative is certainly angled to his point of view, though much more appreciative of the humour in the situation than he can afford to be. But what are we to make of the intervention over the Dante quotation? It is not unlikely that Gino would seek to impress Philip with snippets from the classics learnt by rote, but clearly Forster has other intentions in mind. The authorial comment draws the reader's attention to the quotation. It is 'more apt' than Gino supposes. Why?

A translation of the Italian might read:

> In the middle of the way of our life
> I found myself in a dark wood
> Where the direct road was lost –

– and if we think carefully we should remember that Philip has just gone through a wood on his drive from the station to the town (p. 36). The trees are bare but it is early spring and the ground is covered with violets, although Philip in his preoccupation does not notice them at the time. It seems a place of extraordinary promise, vitality and hope. When next we see it, however, it is in the terrible episode of the abduction and death of the baby (p. 143) where it is dark and muddy, a place of confusion and death. So the wood is a complex symbol that gathers meaning as the text proceeds. It is part of a deeper layer of meaning, what is sometimes termed a 'sub-text', that lies below the amusing social comedy. Forster is giving the reader a clue or hint of this before moving on.

The appropriateness of the quotation to the English visitors should be apparent to us, the readers, if not to them. They are all in the middle of their lives and 'lost' in the midst of confusing experiences. Italy proves to be something of a 'dark wood' in this novel, sometimes exhilarating in its promise of life as Lilia has already found, but sometimes 'dark', dreadful and cruel: Lilia and the baby are to die. Philip, in some senses, is the most lost but also capable of travelling the furthest. He has to explore the dark wood before he can truly grow as a human being. Forster uses Dante's imagery of life as a journey through a place of trial as a serious sub-text beneath the social comedy, and this expands to reveal itself at the end, giving an added dimension to the final chapters. Again, I hope I have shown you how carefully we need to read Forster and pick up the little hints that he gives us. 'The little wood' is another of those details or phrases that recurs to give shape and added significance to the narrative.

I'm going to move on now to look at the parallel scene in the second half of the book, where Philip meets Gino at the opera on his return visit to claim the baby:

He deserted his ladies and plunged towards the box. A young man was flung stomach downwards across the balustrade. Philip handed him up the bouquet and the note. Then his own hands were seized affectionately. It all seemed quite natural.

'Why have you not written?' cried the young man. 'Why do you take me by surprise?'

'Oh, I've written,' said Philip hilariously. 'I left a note this afternoon.'

'Silence! silence!' cried the audience, who were beginning to have enough. 'Let the divine creature continue.' Miss Abbott and Harriet had disappeared.

    'No! no!' cried the young man. 'You don't escape me now.' For Philip was trying feebly to disengage his hands. Amiable youths bent out of the box and invited him to enter it.

    'Gino's friends are ours – '

    'Friends?' cried Gino. 'A relative! A brother! Fra Filippo, who has come all the way from England and never written.'

    'I left a message.'

    The audience began to hiss.

    'Come in to us.'

    'Thank you – ladies – there is not time – '

    The next moment he was swinging by his arms. The moment after he shot over the balustrade into the box. Then the conductor, seeing that the incident was over, raised his baton. The house was hushed, and Lucia di Lammermoor resumed her song of madness and death. (pp. 110–11)

The opera scene is crucial to the design of *Where Angels Fear to Tread* as well as being very funny; it needs careful attention. What Forster is attempting to capture here is the more positive side of Italian life and culture. The opera is a great festive occasion in Italy, but Harriet attempts to spoil the fun by imposing a false sense of order and propriety on the audience. Culture to her is a serious business and she hushes the locals as if she was in church, but, once 'Lucia di Lammermoor' gets underway, she finds that she cannot contain Italian enthusiasm and spontaneity. The excitement mounts to the point of hysteria and, at the end of the 'mad scene' famous for Lucia's demanding aria, some decidedly false and ancient floral tributes descend upon the stage. Though the singer, like the flowers, is past her best, Forster shows very well that it is the spirit of communal celebration, not formal perfection, that lies at the heart of Italian opera. When a *billet-doux* intended for the singer falls into Philip's hands, he gets up to return it, only to discover that the 'innamorato' is none other than Gino himself.

    I feel that Philip's 'desertion' of the English ladies to return the letter is highly suggestive; in a symbolic sense, he has changed sides. The passage is marked by much decided and uninhibited action as Philip is literally dragged protesting over the balustrade into the warm, uncomplicated camaraderie of

Gino and his friends. He plunges towards the box, Gino is 'flung stomach downwards' to seize his hands, swing him and shoot him over the barrier. Philip is transformed by the expansiveness and warmth of the experience; the magic of Italy proves irresistible. English reserve gives way as he becomes 'Fra Filippo' and is claimed as a 'brother'.

However, Forster is too subtle a novelist to let a simple contrast between English inhibition and Italian warmth stand unqualified. In order for Philip to change and grow, he has to take risks, be prepared to stand outside respectable conventions, even behave in an anti-social way. The episode is exhilarating, funny, but also disruptive. Initially co-operative, the audience become restive; finally their patience is exhausted and they begin to hiss. Philip does attempt 'feebly to disengage his hands' and make his excuses. Viewed unsympathetically, his action could be considered rather foolish and impolite. The life that Italy offers Philip through Gino is vital and enriching, but it can be confusing also, its consequences difficult to predict. Even showing us Italy at its most attractive, Forster suggests in all sorts of subtle ways that there is a need and place for discipline, too, in any society. Lucia di Lammermoor's madness and death were brought on by a fatal and doomed love, and her resumed song is a reminder that there are risks and dangers in living fully, or making bold claims on life. It's a small detail, one that you could easily pass over, but it is through such touches that Forster maintains a fine balance between the claims of England and Italy. Both have their positive and negative sides. I think you will find this in almost any passage that you examine.

I'm going to finish my brief examination of the aspects of this novel by looking at its strange conclusion. It will give me an occasion to discuss the two important, and related, aspects of Forster himself: his liberalism and his homosexuality – and how they inform the text. Here is an extract from Caroline and Philip's final conversation on the train returning home when Caroline confesses her love for Gino.

'Don't talk of "faults". You're my friend for ever, Mr Herriton, I think. Only don't be charitable and shift or take the blame. Get over supposing I'm refined. That's what puzzles you. Get over that.'

As she spoke she seemed to be transfigured and to have

indeed no part with refinement or unrefinement any longer. Out of this wreck there was revealed to him something indestructible – something which she, who had given it, could never take away.

'I say again, don't be charitable. If he had asked me, I might have given myself body and soul. That would have been the end of my rescue party. But all through he took me for a superior being – a goddess. I who was worshipping every inch of him, and every word he spoke. And that saved me.'

Philip's eyes were fixed on the Campanile of Airolo. But he saw instead the fair myth of Endymion. This woman was a goddess to the end. For her no love could be degrading: she stood outside all degradation. This episode, which she thought so sordid, and which was so tragic for him, remained supremely beautiful. To such a height was he lifted, that without regret he could now have told her that he was a worshipper too. But what was the use of telling her? For all the wonderful things had happened. (p. 160)

I've said that *Where Angels Fear to Tread* is an 'education' novel, but it's difficult to quantify what it is that Philip has learnt. A less challenging and crudely satisfying end to the novel would have Philip marry Caroline, tell his mother some home truths, and live happily ever after in Italy with Gino as his boon companion. Instead, we end on a note of resignation and defeat. Philip loves Caroline who loves Gino. Nothing is going to happen that changes anyone's life. Sawston triumphs – for 'all the wonderful things had happened'.

I think we've learnt enough of the book by now to see how 'fair' Forster is to everyone's conflicting claims, and fairness is the mark of the good liberal. The reward that the liberal achieves for inactivity is to understand everything; as Philip muses just before this passage: 'nobody but himself would ever see round it now' (p. 160). But that very knowledge, that ability to see and sympathise with all sides of the question, can finally inhibit any action. After all, Endymion, beloved by the moon goddess Selene in the old Greek myth, was lured into perpetual sleep. The consolations for the educated liberal are largely aesthetic and cultural. Forster begins by showing the limitations of Philip's aesthetic view of life, but he doesn't offer him any alternative at the close; indeed, he finishes by endorsing them.

Philip remains locked in that aesthetic appreciation of Caroline as a 'goddess' that we've noted in the earlier passage where she saves him from Gino. This indestructible transfiguration from the wreckage of life is his consolation prize. Knowledge that she loves another is almost a relief; failure becomes a kind of triumph. Only by standing apart can Philip 'see round it all'.

What is true for Philip is also true for Caroline. And this is even more disappointing because she is a stronger, braver person. She is 'saved' by Gino's chivalry from her own physical feelings, but 'saved' in this context is deeply ambiguous. What is she saved for? A life of good works back in Sawston? She is granted, as Philip is, a vision of fulfilment and a measure of self-understanding, but then is 'saved' from commitment to the troublesome uncertainties of a demanding relationship in a foreign land.

It's an odd, painful conclusion but, perhaps, the only honest one for a scrupulous liberal like Forster who understands, all too well, the negative aspects of English bourgeois life, but also appreciates its comforts and security. The sharpness of Forster's satire should not deceive us. We often criticise most acutely what we understand and appreciate most intimately.

What then of Gino and all that he represents? This is where Forster's own, unlocated sexual feelings disturb the text and reinforce, as well as complicate, his liberalism. There is a suggestion, to my mind, that Forster uses Philip to develop a concealed love affair which then has to be 'over-written' by a more conventional one. In other words, Philip loves Gino every bit as much as Caroline does, and in much the same way, but these feelings cannot find direct expression in the text; they have to be masked by Caroline's infatuation and can only surface, disguised, in the scene of disturbing violence between the two men that forms the climax of the action.

The social and cultural values of Italy are a useful measure of the inadequacies of Sawston as we have seen, but Italy is also a country of the mind; its extremes of passion and cruelty act as a private code in this text for the possible gratification of Forster's feared yet longed-for desires – desires that are expressed through Philip's relationship with Gino. Gino's warmth, sexuality, and duplicity are crucial as a focus for all this undeclared feeling. In the end, Philip's desires cannot be admitted, yet neither can Forster go along with any obvious heterosexual

solution. The conventional marriage ending has to be rejected as
dishonest. Erotic repression, so marked a feature of the text as a
whole, gives added poignancy to this, one of his most successful
endings.

4
The Second Italian Novel: *A Room with a View* (1908)

I Constructing an overall analysis

A Room with a View was Forster's third novel to be published but its writing history was a protracted and complex affair. Although the first novel he began, the 'Lucy novel', as he called it, was re-drafted several times and Forster deferred the completion of it twice in order to finish other novels. Maybe because of these difficulties, Forster's own feelings towards this work seem ambivalent: looking back much later he called it his 'nicest novel' and records in his diary at the time that it was 'liked by the young and business men'. This seems like damning with faint praise, but an examination of the plot may help to explain why.

1 *After reading the novel, think about the story and what kind of pattern you can see in the text*

The story opens in Florence. On her 'improving' tour of Italy Lucy Honeychurch arrives at the Pension Bertolini, accompanied by her cousin Charlotte Bartlett, to discover that their rooms do not have a view. Overhearing their disappointment, another resident, Mr Emerson, offers them the rooms of his son George and himself. Though greatly embarrassed by this unorthodox behaviour by social inferiors, they accept after being reassured by Mr Beebe, a clergyman known to them, and shortly to take up the living of Lucy's home parish. The following day Lucy meets the Emersons at the church of Santa Croce where she has been abandoned by an eccentric lady novelist, Miss Lavish, who also lives at the pension. Here, Mr Emerson's frankly secular views cause further embarrassment, and offence to the Reverend Eager, chaplain to the local English community. Events further conspire to bring Lucy and the Emersons together when she witnesses a murder in the Piazza Signoria next day. She faints and is supported by George who accompanies her home. Matters are brought to a crisis during an outing to Fiestole that includes the Emersons. The party is split up and Lucy, seeking the clergymen, finds George instead. He kisses her. Charlotte, who witnesses the kiss, acts the outraged chaperon and both ladies leave Florence at once.

The second half of the novel moves to Summer Street, a small Surrey village where Lucy lives with her mother and brother Freddy in the family home, a house called 'Windy Corner' overlooking the Weald. It is later in the year; Lucy has returned and becomes engaged to Cecil Vyse, a well-connected London aesthete whom she met in Rome. Cecil finds the cheerful domesticity of the Honeychurch household tiresome and irritating; he seeks to rescue Lucy from provincial society and sophisticate her for his artistic pleasure. Playing a mischievous prank, he is responsible for the Emersons renting a house in the village unaware of any past association between Lucy and George. Freddy and George strike up an immediate friendship. In a scene of high comedy they go swimming in a local pool with Mr Beebe and are surprised without their clothes by Cecil, Lucy and her mother. Once again matters are brought to a crisis during a tennis party when George, excited by a literary rendition of his first kiss in one of Miss Lavish's novels, kisses Lucy for a second time. Supported by Charlotte, Lucy ignores his declaration of love and orders him from the house. She breaks off her engagement to Cecil, however.

Though it is clear to the reader that Lucy loves George, she seeks to repress her feelings and plans to travel abroad. By a lucky accident, she meets Mr Emerson at Mr Beebe's rectory although George has already left Summer Street. He divines her true feelings and gives her the courage to declare her love. The novel ends with the newly-wed couple honeymooning in the Pension Bertolini with a view over the river Arno, confident that Lucy's family will eventually forgive them.

What we seem to have here, in outline at least, is a typical plot of young love triumphant over obstacles and difficulties: some of these difficulties are self-imposed, some come from society. It does seem the kind of romantic fiction that would appeal to the immature or conventional reader; I think this is what lies behind Forster's diffidence. On the other hand, some of the greatest novelists have used love and courtship as the motivating force behind their fiction. Forster is working in a great tradition here – Jane Austen immediately comes to mind – and this creates anxieties in a writer. So Forster is vulnerable on two counts. He could be accused of writing a very conventional, unchallenging novel, but his project is also extremely ambitious. This paradox may explain his difficulties in finishing the work. We must remember too that any synopsis of such a novel has severe limitations. A bald account of the greatest love story reduces it to the level of the weakest; it doesn't do justice to the complexity of the psychological analysis or to the discrimination of the moral judgements.

With these thoughts in mind, what can we learn from this basic account? Well, clearly Lucy Honeychurch is the heroine and a very typical kind of heroine she is too, an *ingénue* who has much to learn about the world and about herself. Again, there is the usual conflict in such a romantic story: Lucy has two lovers from very different walks of life and must make a choice between them. This seems to be a story of love triumphing over class. Depending how it is handled it could be trite and sentimental or a searching analysis of a society's values in the manner of Jane Austen. Certainly the antithesis implicit in the title – 'room' and 'view' – is reminiscent of Jane Austen; think of *Pride and Prejudice* or *Sense and Sensibility*. The novel is not called *Lucy Honeychurch* and this implies that Forster is not just interested in Lucy herself but is using her to explore wider moral and social issues. It would seem, even from my short account, that Lucy's two young men represent contrasting values as well as social class, so 'love' might indeed underpin a moral drama. Reminiscent of Jane Austen, too, is Forster's social world, a genteel world of clergymen, spinsters, comfortable family life and the domestic politics of small privileged communities.

The 'shape' of the novel is also of interest and the way that Forster uses Italy. The fiction falls neatly into two halves. We see Lucy abroad and then at home. Italy is where her growth begins, presenting her with challenges to her conventional upbringing that are both liberating and confusing, but back home in England is where her struggles are complicated and must be resolved. Finally, there is Forster's use of names. This also gives us clues to a moral intention. 'Eager' and 'Lavish' certainly seem to signpost something, but 'Honeychurch' is particularly interesting. It is close to being an oxymoron – 'honey' implies sweetness and pleasure, 'church' maybe social discipline and moral control. Anyway, it certainly suggests some unresolved conflict in our heroine.

I think we are now ready to go on to our next step. Lucy is at the centre of this novel and a basic analysis is best achieved by charting her progress through the book.

2   *Select a short passage featuring one of the main characters and try to build upon the ideas you have established so far*

I've decided to look at a passage in the oddly titled 'Fourth Chapter' where Lucy wanders alone, dissatisfied and unchaperoned, into the Piazza Signoria at dusk (page references to the novel relate to the Penguin edition, 1988).

But though she spent nearly seven lire, the gates of liberty seemed still unopened. She was conscious of her discontent; it was new to her to be conscious of it. 'The world,' she thought, 'is certainly full of beautiful things, if only I could come across them.' It was not surprising that Mrs Honeychurch disapproved of music, declaring that it always left her daughter peevish, unpractical, and touchy.

'Nothing ever happens to me,' she reflected, as she entered the Piazza Signoria and looked nonchalantly at its marvels, now fairly familiar to her. The great square was in shadow; the sunshine had come too late to strike it. Neptune was already insubstantial in the twilight, half god, half ghost, and his fountain plashed dreamily to the men and satyrs who idled together on its marge. The Loggia showed as the triple entrance of a cave, wherein dwelt many a deity, shadowy, but immortal, looking forth upon the arrivals and departures of mankind. It was the hour of unreality – the hour, that is, when unfamiliar things are real. An older person at such an hour and in such a place might think that sufficient was happening to him, and rest content. Lucy desired more.

She fixed her eyes wistfully on the tower of the palace, which rose out of the lower darkness like a pillar of roughened gold. It seemed no longer a tower, no longer supported by earth, but some unattainable treasure throbbing in the tranquil sky. Its brightness mesmerized her, still dancing before her eyes when she bent them to the ground and started towards home.

Then something did happen.

Two Italians by the Loggia had been bickering about a debt. 'Cinque lire,' they had cried, 'cinque lire!' They sparred at each other, and one of them was hit lightly upon the chest. He frowned; he bent towards Lucy with a look of interest, as if he had an important message for her. He opened his lips to deliver it, and a stream of red came out between them and trickled down his unshaven chin. (pp. 61–2)

In discussing this and all subsequent passages, I shall follow the same steps that I did in the last chaper but I won't note each individually. So what is the passage about? At one level this is easy to answer: Lucy has become bored and dissatisfied with her life as a protected tourist in Italy and seeks some adventure on her own. While she is in the square a quarrel suddenly erupts in front of her and one of the men is stabbed and killed. I suppose the most obvious tension in the passage is between the violence of the events and the mysterious way that they are presented through Lucy's trance-like state of mind. It is the 'hour of unreality' and the dusk has the effect of making everything insubstantial, questioning its reality and confusing categories. Men and satyrs sit together; Neptune is 'half god, half ghost'. The Loggia becomes a fabulous 'cave' inhabited by 'many a deity' that are 'shadowy, but immortal'. This strange mood is intensified by the tower. Lucy is mesmerised by it; it becomes a thing of great beauty, an 'unattainable treasure', a pillar of gold floating unsupported and 'throbbing' in the evening sunlight. The description of the fight continues in this style. The men spar and one is hit 'lightly'; Lucy doesn't realise what is happening until he turns to her and the blood suddenly runs from his mouth. Because we share Lucy's lack of awareness, the presentation of the dying man, his frown, his 'look of interest' and his 'important message' of blood is both mysterious and very shocking. The violence is so casual and unexpected.

The significance of the episode can best be appreciated by thinking about the events that have led up to it. Lucy has come to Italy to 'improve' herself, to learn about Italian art and culture. Throughout her stay in Florence, she has been cossetted and fussed over by her anxious cousin, Charlotte Bartlett, and other guests at the Pension Bertolini. A mishap which left her abandoned at the church of Santa Croce 'with no Baedeker' (ch. 2) is treated comically as a minor disaster. Without the appropriate guide-book, Lucy doesn't know how to respond to the culture around her. Here she seeks to discover the spirit behind great art by paying seven lire for some photographic reproductions. What is true of art is also true of life. Lucy has been taught to live by convention and not to trust her instincts. The directness of the Emersons alarms and confuses her. We have learnt enough about her already to know that she has energy, spontaneity and much natural charm, but this has been repressed by excessive middle-class caution and can only now find expression in the vigour of her piano playing. There is something rather touching about the innocence that she shows in the first paragraph, and something rather sad too about her 'peevish' complaint that 'nothing ever happens' to her.

The rest of the passage shows Lucy's sudden introduction into the dangers and mysteries that life can offer. After living second-hand through guide-books, chaperones and photographic reproductions, she is suddenly confronted with the raw material of life itself, the extremes of its beauty and violence. Neptune, the satyrs, the fountain, the Loggia, the square and the tower suddenly become more than a scenic view that a tourist might glance at 'nonchalantly'. They seem transformed into the original impulses that went into their making. And those impulses are overwhelming and unpredictable. You might not go along with this, but I sense some initiation into the wonders and perils of passionate sexuality as well as cruelty and death. After all, 'an older person' might well rest content at such a time and in such a place, but Lucy 'desired more'.

The tower rising from the 'lower darkness' into the bright evening sun seems almost too insistently phallic; to me it represents a challenge to Lucy, a sudden manifestation of delight that she turns away from only to confront the dying man. The promise of life gives way to violence and death.

Perhaps it is the fact that sunshine and shadow, beauty and cruelty, passion and death, are inextricably linked that is the 'important message' that the dying man symbolically wishes to tell Lucy. We can only speculate. Remembering the title of the novel, what we can say is that Lucy has been given an extraordinary visionary 'view' of life, and life's possibilities. Significantly it is into George's arms that she collapses immediately after this passage.

Stylistically the passage is most interesting. Forster's writing is deceptively casual but he is attempting ambitious things. He moves quite swiftly from a detached irony that gently mocks Lucy's naîveté – even after spending seven lire 'the gates of liberty seemed still unopened' – to a quite different order of reality. It's not only that he writes more poetically, using words like 'plashed' or figurative language like 'roughened gold', but that he manages to disturb our habitual way of looking at things. The manner in which he suggests the bizarre oddity of death by delaying our understanding of it until the blood comes from the man's mouth is, I think, quite masterly and genuinely disturbing. Let's move on now to another passage.

3 Select a second passage for discussion

'Eccolo!' he exclaimed.

At the same moment the ground gave way, and with a cry she fell out of the wood. Light and beauty enveloped her. She had fallen on to a little open terrace, which was covered with violets from end to end.

'Courage!' cried her companion, now standing some six feet above. 'Courage and love.'

She did not answer. From her feet the ground sloped sharply into the view, and violets ran down in rivulets and streams and cataracts, irrigating the hill-side with blue, eddying round the tree stems, collecting into pools in the hollows, covering the grass with spots of azure foam. But never again were they in such profusion; this terrace was the well-head, the primal source whence beauty gushed out to water the earth.

Standing at its brink, like a swimmer who prepares, was the

good man. But he was not the good man that she had expected, and he was alone.

George had turned at the sound of her arrival. For a moment he contemplated her, as one who had fallen out of heaven. He saw radiant joy in her face, he saw the flowers beat against her dress in blue waves. The bushes above them closed. He stepped quickly forward and kissed her.

Before she could speak, almost before she could feel, a voice called, 'Lucy! Lucy! Lucy!' The silence of life had been broken by Miss Bartlett, who stood brown against the view. (pp. 88–9)

I've chosen this because I feel the drive to Fiestole is the climax of the first part of the novel. Once arrived at this famous tourist 'view' of the Val d'Arno, Lucy finds herself excluded from the companionship of her cousin and Miss Lavish. Somewhat at a loss, she asks the Italian driver to lead her to the 'good men', her feeble attempt in Italian to indicate the clergymen. Instead the driver leads her to George. She falls out of some bushes onto the hillside and George takes her in his arms and kisses her, a kiss that is going to haunt Lucy for the rest of the novel. Any further communication is cut short by the arrival of Charlotte.

As I see it, the tension in the passage is between Lucy and George's 'view' of each other – which is clearly much more than merely a physical view – and the ominous figure of Miss Bartlett who comes to stand obstructively between them and it. Imaginatively, the passage is dominated by images of bright blue water. The violets which cover the bank in such profusion run in 'rivulets and streams and cataracts' 'irrigating' the hillside, 'eddying' round trees, 'collecting into pools' and covering the grass with 'azure foam'. Lucy is seen to fall into a gushing stream, a 'well-head' where beauty pours out to 'water the earth'. The second half of the passage shifts the attention to George and his vision of Lucy but the water imagery is sustained. He stands on the 'brink' of the terrace, 'like a swimmer who prepares', seeing the flowers 'beat against her dress in blue waves.' I am reminded that one of the photographs that Lucy bought in the Piazza Signoria episode I have just discussed was Botticelli's 'Birth of Venus'. Venus, the goddess of love and beauty, was born from the sea just as Lucy is now to George's heightened imagination. To him she seems a goddess 'fallen out of heaven'.

Clearly this water imagery is crucial to Forster's vision. In this context, it seems to stand for life. Lucy, unintentionally, 'falls' into an unstable, but privileged and amazingly beautiful space. You might say that she takes a plunge into life and away from the safety and stability of merely living by convention. George jumps in to join her. You may feel that this is rather an odd way of putting it but, for me, it is the sense of the passage. This space is mental and emotional, private to those who discover it. It is also extremely fragile; the ominously 'brown' presence of Charlotte and her possessive call immediately destroys this 'silence of life'.

If I think about how the novel has developed up to this point, I can see that this is the last and most dramatic episode in Lucy's Italian education, a private, emotional education that poor Charlotte could hardly approve of. First Lucy was exposed to the challenging, socially unorthodox Emersons at the pension and at Santa Croce; then she was given an insight into the potential and danger of life in the Piazza Signoria, and now she has been thrust into a vision of love's joys by George's kiss. This culminating episode is part of a sequence of significant events that have determined the shape of the first part of this novel.

I suppose an unsympathetic reader might feel the passage is rather over-written. It's important when reading Forster to catch the right tone. My feeling is that it is playfully serious. Forster is enjoying the full-blown romanticism of his vision but certain ironies keep it in check and in relationship with the real world. Even in this most lyrical of passages, the narrator maintains control and a certain detachment over his own out-pourings. For example, there is the use of the Italian driver and the serious use made of comic misunderstandings. In a height-ened, stylised mode, more like an opera than a realistic novel, the driver first uses Italian – 'Eccolo!' (There he is!) – and then changes to English for his final exhortation: 'Courage and love'. Then there is the complex pun on the idea of 'the good men'. This is the source of comic misunderstanding but also makes a serious moral point, a point that has been built up to throughout the first part of the novel. Who are indeed the 'good men'? The clergymen that convention insists must be good, or those troublesome, unconventional Emersons? Perhaps Italians have an intuitive wisdom in such matters denied to the English? In such ways Forster keeps the mind of the reader alert as well as stimulating the imagination.

I think it would be useful now to go on and look at a passage in

the second part of the novel where Lucy is with the other man in
her life, her fiancé, Cecil Vyse.

4   Select a third passage for discussion

'Up to now I have never kissed you.'
She was as scarlet as if he had put the thing most inde-
licately.
'No – more you have,' she stammered.
'Then I ask you – may I now?'
'Of course you may, Cecil. You might before. I can't run at
you, you know.'
At that supreme moment he was conscious of nothing but
absurdities. Her reply was inadequate. She gave such a
business-like lift to her veil. As he approached her he found
time to wish that he could recoil. As he touched her, his gold
pince-nez became dislodged and was flattened between them.
Such was the embrace. He considered, with truth, that it
had been a failure. Passsion should believe itself irresistible. It
should forget civility and consideration and all other curses of
a refined nature. Above all, it should never ask for leave
where there is a right of way. Why could he not do as any
labourer or navvy – nay, as any young man behind the
counter would have done? He recast the scene. Lucy was
standing flower-like by the water; he rushed up and took her
in his arms; she rebuked him, permitted him, and revered
him ever after for his manliness. For he believed that women
revere men for their manliness.
They left the pool in silence, after this one salutation. He
waited for her to make some remark which should show him
her inmost thoughts. At last she spoke, and with fitting
gravity.
'Emerson the name was, not Harris.'
'What name?'
'The old man's.'
'What old man?'
'That old man I told you about. The one Mr Eager was so
unkind to.'
He could not know that this was the most intimate conversation they had ever had. (pp. 127–8)

This passage is taken from Chapter 9, quite early on in the second part of the novel. The engaged pair are wandering alone in a wood near Lucy's home and, by a pool where Lucy used to swim as a child, Cecil asks for his first kiss: it is not a success. This is an amusing episode – up to a point; there's a comic disparity between Cecil's elevated notions of how this event should have gone and the clumsy, rather feeble reality.

Paradoxically it is the polite, detached formality of Cecil's request that makes it seem so indecent. He is going through the forms of passion rather than being compelled by passion itself. Lucy intuits this and it makes her embarrassed, stiff and similarly formal. She blushes, stammers, and is unromantically 'business-like'. This, of course, makes him even more inhibited. He feels as if he is acting an absurd part, and so, of course, he is. Good manners aping passion is an absurd sight. Cecil is going through the conventional form of what fiancés are supposed to want to do. Freddy's use of the family joke by calling him 'the fiasco' (p. 114) is entirely appropriate; as a newly engaged lover, that's exactly what he is. The squashed pince-nez sums it all up. The title of this chapter is called 'Lucy as a work of Art' and Cecil is a rather bookish character who can only handle life by viewing it through the spectacles of art. When he tries to engage with life directly, he comes to grief. It is significant that after the failed kiss he recasts the whole sequence again, turning it into a day-dream or romantic fantasy. He is transformed into a masterful lover and Lucy standing 'flower-like' by the water cannot but respond and revere his 'manliness'. Of course this fantasy resembles George's kiss in reality – or, we feel, could easily have done, if Charlotte had not intervened.

What Lucy's thoughts are on the matter and what invidious comparisons she might be making are not open to us directly. If Cecil is right, she should be revering George secretly for his 'manliness'. I think we can infer the true state of affairs from her muted conversation at the end of the passage. She has talked about the Emersons to her family but, seeking to evade their reality, she disguised them under the name of 'Harris'. As I see it, Cecil's kiss recalls the genuine passion of George. By confessing the false name, Lucy is attempting to be honest about her past and come to terms with it. It's a kind of covert appeal to Cecil, but he cannot appreciate the importance of the confession, so Lucy must remain emotionally muddled and confused.

It is clear that this kiss and the general situation in which it occurs are deliberately designed to recall the first kiss. It's a parallel scene intended to draw attention to the contrast between Lucy's two lovers. In both cases Lucy is seen and desired in a natural context; here it is the favourite woods of her childhood, in Italy it was the bank of violets. George was able to respond to the 'view', that vision of living beauty which Lucy was but a part. In a conversation leading up to this kiss, Lucy and Cecil have a discussion about rooms and views. She tells him that she can only think of him 'in a room' with 'no view'. Rather hurt, he tells her that he always thinks of her in a view, but we know this to be the rather fantastic 'artistic' backdrop to a Leonardo painting (p. 108). Cecil cannot respond directly to nature as Lucy and George can. He hasn't got 'a view'; his love of culture blinds him, hence the significance of the crushed pince-nez. The result, as we have just seen, is that he is unable to experience spontaneous feeling.

Stylistically the last passage was lyrical and poetic. This is much more conventional in its use of dialogue and an overall narrator who is detached from the action yet can also enter into Cecil's thoughts. The narrator here is sharply observant in a social way, unlike the previous piece, but handles the scene with a complex mixture of judgement and sympathy. The decision to exclude the reader from Lucy's thoughts at this point is, I think, a wise one: it makes her dilemma more interesting. Cecil, on the other hand, is certainly more fully realised – more intimately known – than George was, and this may be true of Forster's treatment of the pair overall. It is something worth following up. Forster captures well Cecil's complex attitude towards spontaneous passion and 'manliness'; he seems to see these things as the product of simple-minded ignorance or vulgarity. There's a complex mixture here of envy and snobby distaste for labourers, navvies and counter-jumpers. Cecil seems much more socially 'placed' than George is and so a much stronger character. If this is true overall, it could be a source of weakness in the book.

How does Lucy solve her problem? To make some progress on this, we need to look at a passage near the end of the novel.

5   *Select a fourth passage for discussion*

She turned to Mr Emerson in despair. But his face revived
her. It was the face of a saint who understood.
'Now it is all dark. Now Beauty and Passion seem never to
have existed. I know. But remember the mountains over
Florence and the view. Ah, dear, if I were George, and gave
you one kiss, it would make you brave. You have to go cold
into a battle that needs warmth, out into the muddle that you
have made yourself; and your mother and all your friends will
despise you, oh my darling, and rightly, if it is ever right to
despise. George still dark, all the tussle and the misery without
a word from him. Am I justified?' Into his own eyes tears
came. 'Yes, for we fight for more than Love or Pleasure: there
is Truth. Truth counts, Truth does count.'
'You kiss me,' said the girl. 'You kiss me. I will try.'
He gave her a sense of deities reconciled, a feeling that, in
gaining the man she loved, she would gain something for the
whole world. Throughout the squalor of her homeward drive
– she spoke at once – his salutation remained. He had robbed
the body of its taint, the world's taunts of their sting; he had
shown her the holiness of direct desire. She 'never exactly
understood,' she would say in after years, 'how he managed to
strengthen her. It was as if he had made her see the whole of
everything at once.' (p. 225)

I've chosen this passage, partly because it includes another very
significant kiss, but also because it seems to be the climax of the
whole novel. It is the end of the penultimate chapter where Lucy
comes across Mr Emerson in the vicarage, just before her
departure to Greece. Though she has got rid of Cecil by this
stage, she is still running away from her problems. Mr Emerson
sees into the heart of her self-deception and gives her the
courage to marry George, a socially undesirable match that will
offend her family and friends. The tension is clearly between
her fears and Mr Emerson's almost mystic optimism.

Though you are unlikely to notice them all at first reading,
this passage picks up arguments, words, phrases and images that
have been used with gathering significance throughout the
novel. Life has been seen as a battle between light and dark,
honesty and lies, spontaneity and convention, 'views' and

'rooms'. There is always a struggle between these two opposing forces and very few win out to find some form of self-integrity. Most join what Forster calls 'the vast armies of the benighted' (p. 194). Lucy nearly does but is saved just in time by Mr Emerson's intervention.

This idea of life as some kind of testing moral struggle is picked up by the use of such words as 'brave', 'battle', 'fight', 'tussle', 'taunts', 'sting', and 'strengthen'. Lucy's fight for self-clarification is a private, moral crusade, but we are asked to believe that its outcome has implications for society as a whole: she feels that 'gaining the man she loved, she would gain something for the whole world'. This gives the passage an elevated, evangelical tone that you might feel is at odds with a story of social comedy and young love. Thinking further, however, you might also realise that such sententiousness is a part of Forster's narrative tone overall and does recur amongst the satire and the lyrical symbolism we've already noted. Forster's moral concern is signposted clearly enough in the chapter headings of Part 2; 'Lying to George', 'Lying to Cecil', 'Lying to Mr Beebe' . . . , etc. Lucy has been in a 'muddle', the word is a loaded one for Forster and has been used repeatedly through-out the book, and now she must sort herself out.

Old Mr Emerson has a special role in this respect. At the very beginning of the novel, he offered Lucy a 'room with a view', first literally, and then by challenging her petty Edwardian conventionality. Now, begging her to remember the wider vistas of that Italian experience – 'remember the mountains over Florence and the view' – he leads her out of her moral darkness and finally manages to make her see 'the whole of everything at once'. Throughout the novel, he has been something of a 'holy fool', a rather bumbling, sententious, old man but now we are asked to see him as 'a saint who understood'. The narrator elevates him into a kind of mystic seer who has the power to unite what in the world are always seen as contraries – personal desire and public duty. He shows Lucy the 'holiness of direct desire' – that 'love' can be linked to 'Truth' – and by insisting that the search for one must lead to the other, he convinces her that these apparently irreconcilable 'deities' can be reconciled. Mr Emerson preaches a new morality based on personal integrity that will advance society as a whole. His magical kiss 'robs the world's taunts of their sting' and gives Lucy the ability to reconcile the conflicting impulses of desire and morality inscribed in her name – 'Honeychurch'.

It's clear that a very personal morality is being expressed directly through Mr Emerson here, and that the narrator's detachment from his character has been lost. Instead of satire or poetry the tone is more one of the pulpit with a lot of grand abstraction and serious insistence: 'Truth counts, Truth does count'. This is a sermon showing the need for a new, true religion of personal relationships to triumph over the false conventional one of respectability and outward appearances. It presents a challenge to the reader in that it seems to break free from its surrounding fictional context.

Clearly this confronts us with some problems. Perhaps we feel that Lucy has been let off the hook too easily. Experience tells us that life's moral dilemmas aren't to be so easily solved by the timely intervention of magical helpers. The narrator's claim that Mr Emerson's face is one of 'a saint who understood' is a bold one and difficult to support, while we might feel justifiably aggrieved that Lucy 'never exactly understood' how she found the courage to change her life. As the centre of the book's moral struggle, perhaps she should. You could say Lucy has been eased through the cruel responsibility of making her own decision and this leads to a rather glib happy ending. True, this is in the spirit of conventional, romantic comedy and gives us pleasure at the time but, considered afterwards, it may seem less satisfactory. It is perhaps too conventional, too neat, to support the rather unconventional attitudes that the book expresses as a whole.

I've now looked at four widely spaced passages that deal with Lucy's growth into personal awareness. I think it's time to take stock of the progress I've made so far in my basic analysis by asking myself the final question:

6   *Have I achieved a sufficiently complex sense of the novel?*

I think that I've made significant if, in some ways, rather limited progress. I do have a better grasp of the basic narrative organisation of the story and some understanding of Lucy's development as a character, though not enough; I would need to examine some more passages to get a better grasp of that. For example, I've some appreciation now of how Forster uses Italy to further Lucy's development because I've seen her as a tourist in the first part of the novel, but I have no real sense of her in England or in her family context. Certainly I understand a little more about the suggestive symbolism of 'rooms' and 'views' and how Forster uses it to develop his moral vision, but I've not got much material yet on how Forster uses the Emersons to provide Lucy with 'views' or how others seek to trap her in 'rooms'. There's a whole range of minor characters and some substantial ones like Charlotte Bartlett and Mr Beebe to look at, both in relation to Lucy and their role in the novel generally.

The work I've done so far has helped me get a sense of what Forster's moral values might be in this novel but only in a sketchy way. Just how much there is still to do is evident in the chapter headings. These do indicate areas in Forster's narrative strategy that I've yet to consider and make sense of. Some are self-explanatory and point to the plot; others, particularly in the second part, do not. For example the opening chapter of Part 2 is called 'Medieval' and the concluding chapter is called 'The End of the Middle Ages'. The relevance of these chapter headings to Lucy's story isn't at all clear but there has to be an important signficance attached to them. Also mysteriously named is 'Twelfth Chapter' which seems to be placed in significant parallel to the strange 'Fourth Chapter' in Part 1, an extract from which we've discussed, where Lucy was introduced to the mysteries of life and death.

We began this chapter by considering the rather traditional, even old-fashioned, nature of this novel, with its interest in the courtship and marriage of a young girl, but such chapter headings seem to set up interesting complications; they suggest that the overall design of the book is not so clear-cut or as simple as it appears at first. It's some of these more oblique and apparently marginal aspects of the novel that I want to examine in the second part of this chapter.

II Aspects of the novel

I'm going to begin by looking at a passage involving old Mr Emerson, Mr Eager and Lucy in Chapter 2.

'Remember,' he was saying, 'the facts about this church of Santa Croce; how it was built by faith in the full fervour of medievalism before any taint of the Renaissance had appeared. Observe how Giotto in these frescoes – now, unhappily, ruined by restoration – is untroubled by the snares of anatomy and perspective. Could anything be more majestic, more pathetic, beautiful, true? How little, we feel, avails knowledge and technical cleverness against a man who truly feels!'

'No!' exclaimed Mr Emerson, in much too loud a voice for church. 'Remember nothing of the sort! Built by faith indeed! That simply means the workmen weren't paid properly. And as for the frescoes, I see no truth in them. Look at that fat man in blue! He must weigh as much as I do, and he is shooting into the sky like an air-balloon.'

He was referring to the fresco of the Ascension of St John. Inside, the lecturer's voice faltered, as well it might. The audience shifted uneasily, and so did Lucy. She was sure that she ought not to be with these men; but they had cast a spell over her. They were so serious and so strange that she could not remember how to behave. (pp. 43–4)

This exchange occurs when Lucy, abandoned by Miss Lavish and without her guide-book, wanders into the church of Santa Croce and meets the Emersons. When she asks to be shown the Giotto frescoes, they happen to overhear Mr Eager's talk on the subject. Mr Emerson's spontaneous comments are far too loud and interrupt the lecture, much to Lucy's embarrassment. Superficially at least, this is a comic conflict between Mr Eager's academic, religious views and Mr Emerson's forthright common sense.

Mr Eager, as his name implies, is a rather humourless, dogmatic lecturer. His praise for all things medieval at the expense of the Renaissance reveals a narrowly religious and ascetic personality. The church has been built in 'fervour' and 'by faith' before the 'taint' of a more secular view of the world. In effect, Eager praises Giotto for his ignorance of modern anatomy and perspective because they are distracting 'snares' drawing the attention away from God and on to man. Quite misguidedly, he praises Giotto for his childlike faith and technical incompetence, and so, incidentally, reveals in himself a lack of understanding in the principles of medieval art. His dislike of the Renaissance is not based on any artistic judgement but on his hatred of the Renaissance's celebration of the human body and its progressive interest in all secular things. These attributes he dismisses as merely informed, unfeeling, 'technical cleverness'.

Mr Emerson's blunt retort, given without any rhetorical flourishes, de-mystifies the labour involved in any human endeavour and shows the simple human feeling that Mr Eager praises academically, but significantly fails to show in his own life. Mr Emerson values truth over art and reveals a defiant ignorance of aesthetics and artistic convention. Rather like a small child, his naïve directness is both embarrassing and very amusing. It exposes Mr Eager's posturing and empty pretention for what it is. Above all, in this outburst Mr Emerson shows himself passionately concerned with the things of this world rather than the next. The passage closes with the ambiguous effect of all this on Lucy. Her own reliance and acceptance of convention has been challenged. 'She could not remember how to behave'. She feels uneasy at being associated with the Emersons and yet something in her can't help but respond to them: 'they had cast a spell over her'.

One important aspect of this passage is its contribution to a complex, on-going argument or debate in the book between the respective merits of art and life, where an excessive concern for the outward forms of art is shown to hinder or become a substitute for full, spontaneous living; the narrow religious view of art that Eager displays here shows an attitude of mind that is content to observe life rather than get involved in it. It's a characteristic he shares with the timid tourists he lectures. Remember the first passage that we looked at? There we saw Lucy attempting, like a tourist, to buy experience through photographs of great paintings before she is suddenly made aware of the mysterious powers of life and death that lie behind such marketed reproductions. The value of art in this narrow, appropriating sense is seen as highly suspect; 'art appreciation' can degenerate into just another set of rules or falsifying conventions that can be used to separate people, encourage them to be dishonest about their feelings and draw them away from their real needs. Art may enrich life but it is no substitute for it. Excessive concern for the outward forms of beauty can limit our capacity for ordinary human feeling. In the first part of the novel, both Mr Eager and Miss Lavish demonstrate this, amusing though the latter is in her tireless search for 'dear dirty back ways' (p. 36) as local colour for her romantic novels.

But Forster's use of art is detailed and moves beyond this more general point. As we see here, he sets up a fairly arbitrary conflict between the spirit of medievalism and the Renaissance to extol the claims of the body over those of the spirit. The spirit without the body is shown to be narrow, possessive and ungenerous. Mr Eager praises medieval art at the expense of the Renaissance, but Lucy, a little later in this scene, has a sudden vision of George as a Michelangelo figure, 'healthy and muscular', like one of the portraits on the roof of the Sistine chapel (p. 45); Michelangelo's ceiling is, of course, one of the glories of the Renaissance. In contrast, here is our first description of Cecil early in Part 2 in the chapter entitled 'Medieval':

> Appearing thus late in the story, Cecil must be at once described. He was medieval. Like a Gothic statue. Tall and refined, with shoulders that seemed braced square by an effort of will, and a head that was tilted a little higher than the usual level of vision, he resembled those fastidious saints who guard the portals of a French cathedral. Well educated, well endowed, and not deficient physically, he remained in the grip of a certain devil whom the modern world knows as self-consciousness, and whom the medieval, with dimmer vision, worshipped as asceticism. A Gothic statue implies celibacy, just as a Greek statue implies fruition, and perhaps this was what Mr Beebe meant. And Freddy, who ignored history and art, perhaps meant the same when he failed to imagine Cecil wearing another fellow's cap. (pp. 105–6)

Now this might seem a rather odd way to introduce an important new character unless you have some understanding of Forster's overall strategy in the text. There is certainly no attempt to describe Cecil realistically, instead we have this exaggerated, grotesque picture of him as a 'Gothic' statue. This portrayal of him is clearly intended to contrast him with the physically robust George. But of course the description gains additional force and meaning once you have picked up the conflict between medieval and Renaissance art generally that runs through the text. For Forster, Renaissance art, like the

Greek statues praised here, 'implies fruition' and celebrates life. It is Renaissance art that stirs Lucy's rebellion in the Piazza Signoria and later, kissed by George in a sea of blue violets, like Botticelli's Venus she is born into life.

By describing Cecil in this unnatural way, Forster is clearly setting him alongside characters like Eager and Miss Lavish who value the appearance of art rather than the substance of life: remember that Cecil seeks to transform Lucy into a Leonardo painting just as Miss Lavish turns her into a conventional, *ingénue* heroine in one of her silly novels. The whole stress of the description is on Cecil's retreat from life to become some sort of rigid art-object that has lost all human contours. There is a sense of willed perversity in this attempt, the shoulders 'braced square', the head 'tilted' unnaturally high, that is reminiscent of Eager's description of the Giotto frescoes that we have just discussed. Like them, Cecil is denied normal anatomy and perspective. The narrator's attitude is clear; Cecil is in the 'grip of a certain devil' that seeks to reject the body. 'Grip' is a significant word that recalls Cecil's surname, Vyse; Vyse suggests vice with its implications of perversion and unnatural force, but also the word vie, meaning proud and competing – which is what Cecil is as a rival for Lucy's hand. Mr Beebe's earlier remark that 'Mr Vyse is an ideal bachelor' (p. 104) and Freddy's instinctive dislike of Cecil's lack of warmth and generosity only confirm what Forster's imagery has already told us.

Note also that Cecil is symbolically seen as guarding the portal or doorway of a cathedral, which is, after all, an enormous religious room. This suggests to me that he is thus seen as inviting Lucy into an enclosing, exclusive, spiritual relationship and so appealing to the 'churchly' aspect in her nature that is implied in her name. This idea of enclosing guardianship is also used by Forster to suggest other menacing attributes of Cecil's 'medievalism'. Chivalry is a virtue of the medieval knight and its patronising over-protective modern version is something that Lucy alternately runs to or seeks to escape throughout the novel. In this way, Cecil can be seen as one of a number of chaperones or false guardians, male and female, who seek to deny Lucy the freedom to discover her own nature. Of these, Charlotte Bartlett and Mr Beebe are the most dangerous, because the most complex; Forster's treatment of them is something I'd like briefly to consider by looking at a passage much later in the novel.

'It is absolutely necessary,' she continued, lowering her veil and whispering through it with passion, an intensity, that surprised him. 'I know – I *know*.' The darkness was coming on, and he felt that this odd woman really did know. 'She must not stop here a moment, and we must keep quiet till she goes. I trust that the servants know nothing. Afterwards – but I may have said too much already. Only, Lucy and I are helpless against Mrs Honeychurch alone. If you help, we may succeed. Otherwise – '

'Otherwise – ?'

'Otherwise,' she repeated, as if the word held finality.

'Yes, I will help her,' said the clergyman, setting his jaw firm. 'Come, let us go back now, and settle the whole thing up.'

Miss Bartlett burst into florid gratitude. The tavern sign – a beehive trimmed evenly with bees – creaked in the wind outside as she thanked him. Mr Beebe did not quite understand the situation; but then he did not desire to understand it, nor jump to the conclusion of 'another man' that would have attracted a grosser mind. He only felt that Miss Bartlett knew of some vague influence from which the girl desired to be delivered, and which might well be clothed in the fleshly form. Its very vagueness spurred him into knight-errantry. His belief in celibacy, so reticent, so carefully concealed beneath his tolerance and culture, now came to the surface and expanded like some delicate flower. 'They that marry do well, but they that refrain do better.' So ran his belief, and he never heard that an engagement was broken off but with a slight feeling of pleasure. In the case of Lucy, the feeling was intensified through dislike of Cecil; and he was willing to go further – to place her out of danger until she could confirm her resolution to virginity. The feeling was very subtle and quite undogmatic, and he never imparted it to any other of the characters in this entanglement. Yet it existed, and it alone explains his action subsequently, and his influence on the action of the others. The compact that he made with Miss Bartlett in the tavern was to help not only Lucy, but religion also.

They hurried home through a world of black and grey.
(pp. 206–7)

This passage not only shows Forster's strengths as a novelist of
'manners' – or social observation – but that he is always capable
of suggesting something deeper in human character and human
motivation. At this stage in the novel Lucy has broken off with
Cecil; Charlotte and Mr Beebe are conspiring together to help
her escape from George, and her own feelings, by running off to
Greece.

The writing seems simple enough but it is packed with
implication and meaning. Charlotte's characterisation is one of
Forster's great triumphs in the novel, comic and pathetic by
turns, but here seen as sinister, even evil. She is dramatically
presented with her lowered veil and conspiratorial whisper. By
plotting against George, these two are intriguing against life
itself. Charlotte's unnatural, spinsterish repression is well captured. We remember she stood 'brown against the view' in the
second passage we looked at, and here she becomes 'florid',
unnaturally 'blossoming' in her gratitude when she has enlisted
Mr Beebe to her cause.

The portrayal of Mr Beebe is more subtle still. For most of the
book he has seemed to be Lucy's ally and on the side of life. He
has been protective of Lucy but also appreciative of her qualities
and no friend of Cecil's. So much so that his hostility to her and
George at the end comes as a surprise. But Forster has prepared
the way with several delicate touches and this passage is one of
them. We can see that Beebe is tainted with 'medievalism' and as
a clergyman, however superficially worldly he may appear,
remains committed to the spirit at the expense of the body. This
is indicated by the Biblical quotation from Corinthians praising
celibacy. Forster's attitude to this seems deeply ambiguous
because Beebe's belief in celibacy is expressed in the beautiful
image of the expanding, delicate flower. Though superficially
Cecil's enemy, Beebe shares with him that kind of chivalry or
'knight-errantry' that Forster feels is actually destructive of
Lucy's best potential and happiness, because it seeks to enclose,
expropriate and over-protect.

Other symbolic overtones include the weather that lowers its
veil much as Charlotte does. The darkness comes on during the
conversation, the wind makes the tavern sign creak ominously

and the conspirators leave in a world of 'black and grey' that contrasts with Charlotte's 'florid gratitude'. This kind of symbolism is unobtrusive but always present in the novel. The first part is generally bright and sunny but a thunderstorm signals George's defeat before Charlotte hustles Lucy away to Rome. Similarly the second part begins in brilliant sunshine but the landscape, both physical and mental, gets greyer and greyer as Lucy gets progressively more muddled.

Finally, there seems to be some symbolic significance in Beebe's name – I can't believe it accidental that these two meet under a tavern sign showing a beehive 'trimmed evenly with bees'. One must always be careful not to be over-ingenious when examining potential symbolism, but the language does seem to be pointing to something here. Mr Beebe is 'being a bee' – in this instance drawing sustenance from Charlotte's 'florid gratitude' – but the implications are wider than this. Bees in classical and medieval times were often associated with industry and celibacy. They also make honey and so were associated with flattery. Beebe is certainly honey mouthed but, like a bee, also has a secret sting when he is finally thwarted. Perhaps one should not lean too hard on any of these associations but, taken together, they do combine to make a powerful contribution to our sense of Beebe's complexity as a character.

It's with Beebe partly in mind, and my sense of something powerful and unacknowledged working in the text that has nothing much to do with Lucy's problems, that I want to turn finally to the bathing scene in 'Twelfth Chapter'. Here is an extract from it:

'Apooshoo, apooshoo, apooshoo,' went Freddy, swimming for two strokes in either direction, and then becoming involved in reeds or mud.

'Is it worth it?' asked the other, Michelangelesque on the flooded margin.

The bank broke away, and he fell into the pool before he had weighed the question properly.

'Hee – poof – I've swallowed a polly-wog. Mr Beebe, water's wonderful, water's simply ripping.'

'Water's not so bad,' said George, reappearing from his plunge, and spluttering at the sun.

'Water's wonderful. Mr Beebe, do.'

'Apooshoo, kouf.'

Mr Beebe, who was hot, and who always acquiesced where possible, looked around him. He could detect no parishioners except the pine trees, rising steeply on all sides, and gesturing to each other against the blue. How glorious it was! The world of motor-cars and Rural Deans receded illimitably. Water, sky, evergreens, a wind – these things not even the seasons can touch, and surely they lie beyond the intrusion of man?

'I may as well wash too'; and soon his garments made a third little pile on the sward, and he too asserted the wonder of the water.

It was ordinary water, nor was there very much of it, and, as Freddy said, it reminded one of swimming in a salad. The three gentlemen rotated in the pool breast high, after the fashion of the nymphs in Götterdammerung. But either because the rain had given a freshness, or because the sun was shedding the most glorious heat, or because two of the gentlemen were young in years and the third young in the spirit – for some reason or other a change came over them, and they began to play. Mr Beebe and Freddy splashed each other. A little deferentially, they splashed George. He was quiet: they feared they had offended him. Then all the forces of youth burst out. He smiled, flung himself at them, splashed them, ducked them, kicked them, muddied them, and drove them out of the pool. (pp. 149–50)

This idyll in the Surrey countryside seems suggestively similar to the Italian scene we looked at earlier where George kisses Lucy. It may be presented more light-heartedly but in both cases the characters give way to natural impulses in a privileged free space away from social restraint and censure. In both episodes the writing is playful, lyrical and celebratory; it seeks to disrupt and disturb the mundane and everyday. Here we have some most delightful touches of burlesque with the three naked Edwardian men rotating in a diminutive, weed-filled pool like the nymphs from Wagner's Götterdammerung.

Earlier Lucy refers to the place as 'the Sacred Lake' (p. 126) and it is presented here as a kind of pastoral Arcadia – an idealised rural setting where nature is always kind, and men and women can escape from the evils of society. Grass is 'sward', weeds are 'salad', the sun is shedding 'the most glorious heat', and the place lies beyond seasonal change or, hopefully, 'the intrusion of man'. Motor cars and Rural Deans, commerce and class, duty and authority, have no place in it. By putting off their clothes, these men have put away all such worldly considerations. The sacred pool is a place of innocence and childhood. This is emphasised by the use of slangy or infantile language – 'polly-wog', 'simply ripping' – or the reduction of language to cheerful noise – 'apooshoo', 'kouf', 'poof'.

Another obvious link with the Fiestole episode is the baptism into life that the passage suggests, for both make extensive use of water imagery. Standing by the edge of the flowery bank, George was likened to 'a swimmer who prepares'; here, like Lucy then, he falls reluctantly into a beautiful experience expressed in terms that are liquid and aqueous. The effect of this in the first passage was to release sexual passion; here there is much male 'ragging' and horse play, much splashing and spreading of water, that also implies a release of inhibition and sexual energy. Certainly the effect on George is wholly beneficial; released from his gloom 'the forces of youth burst out' leading to a great display of high spirits. Another pointer in the passage is the adjective 'Michelangelesque' applied to George. In the light of our discussion of Forster's use of art, it puts George firmly on the side of vitality and life while, paradoxically, idealising him into the perfect male youth, worthy to be worshipped by the other two with deference.

So we can see that the passage works in parallel with Lucy and George's scene in the first part of the novel, but it also contrasts with it in some very significant ways. The high spirits shown here are exclusively male and seem strangely excessive. Such a scene, both magical and marginal, is rather at odds with the general pattern of the text. It suggests an outbreak of imaginative energy on Forster's part that is not being satisfactorily accommodated elsewhere, a need to celebrate masculine flirtation and camaraderie in a manner that declares its power and sexual appeal while simultaneously masking and concealing these things. Remember this passage is taken from 'Twelfth Chapter', clearly named to place it in significant parallel with 'Fourth Chapter' in Part 1. Both chapters seem to be concerned with sexual and emotional awareness. Just as Lucy was awakened into the wonders and brutality of sexuality there, so here, all the men seem to be initiated into a quite different set of sexual and emotional possibilities. You might feel such feelings are an unnecessary complication in a novel that is supposed to be concerned with heterosexual romance but, of course, such ambiguity can also be a source of enriching strength.

This is particularly true in the added dimension this scene gives to Mr Beebe. He is a transformed character from the one that we saw in the last passage, or the repressive 'long black column' (p. 224) who rebukes Lucy in the penultimate chapter. Here he is a figure of fun but also a figure of great sympathy as he, too, succumbs to the 'wonder of the water' and becomes 'young in spirit'. This transformation does not last, however, for by the next morning the pool has shrunk and lost its glory. As the narrator observes rather ambiguously, the event had been 'a passing benediction whose influence did not pass' (p. 152). The consequence of this is that later, when Beebe, as we have seen, becomes a figure of intrigue and repression, a complicated undertow has been set up in the text that works against the usual expectations of such a novel. Beneath the surface of this conventional love story it is possible to discern a very different kind of romance that makes Beebe's sudden hostility to Lucy all too understandable. I'm inclined to view the power behind this scene as a coded protest then; it registers Forster's dissatisfaction with the patterns and conventions demanded by the heterosexual romantic novel and its necessarily exclusive conclusion; such conventions are too repressive and inadequate to satisfy his needs. This may well be another reason for Forster's disparagement of the novel that we noted at the start of this chapter. There does seem to be an element of impatience in the conclusion.

As I suggested earlier, you also might feel that the ending is too sudden and too neat. The lovers are poorly visualised as a couple; they seem to have reached their happiness too fast and are quite cut off from the society in which they will have to make it last. To compensate, Forster surrounds them with an aura of poetry and mythology. By subsuming them into the roaring flood of the river Arno in the final paragraph, they become a symbol of life's continuity, their 'passion requited, love attained' but, Forster adds, 'they were conscious of a love more mysterious than this': complex, unaccommodated characters, Beebe particularly, but also Cecil who is quite sympathetically treated after Lucy's rejection, and even poor Charlotte, press in from the margins of this text, their needs, the challenges they present, unmet and unanswered.

5
The First English Novel:
The Longest Journey (1907)

I Constructing an overall analysis

The Longest Journey is the first of two novels entirely set in England; it is also the most puzzling and complex of Forster's early novels and the one for which he had most affection. Whatever other novels you have to study, if you want to get closer to Forster himself, this is the book to read. It is a curious fiction and not often rated as an unqualified success but it is the most intimate of Forster's major works and, in some ways, the most bold and ambitious. He takes more imaginative risks here than elsewhere, and engages most directly with his private obsessions and preoccupations, his hopes and fears. It is also the most autobiographical of his novels, as I think a synopsis will show.

1 *After reading the novel, think about the story and what kind of pattern you can see in the text*

The story opens in Rickie Elliot's undergraduate rooms in Edwardian Cambridge; while he day-dreams, Stuart Ansell and other friends debate the nature of reality. Their discussion is interrupted by Agnes Pembroke, invited with her brother Herbert for a visit. Ansell rudely ignores her, declaring later that she doesn't really exist. After the Pembrokes' departure, we learn that Rickie's childhood has been unhappy and lonely. He idealised his mother but his hated father despised both wife and son. (Like his father, Rickie has a club foot.) Neither had any chance of a fulfilling life together while he lived, and expectations of better times after his death were cruelly cut short by Rickie's mother's own death a few days later.

During the Christmas vacation, Rickie visits the Pembrokes at Sawston, a genteel town in the south of England. Herbert teaches at a minor public school there. Agnes is engaged to Gerald Dawes, an athletic bully from Rickie's own schooldays. However, Rickie idealises the lovers when he sees them embrace unaware, and so is able to comfort Agnes when Gerald dies suddenly after a footballing accident. Rickie returns to Cambridge and becomes engaged to Agnes when she visits him during his final term. Ansell is disgusted and warns Rickie against her, prophesying disaster.

The scene shifts to Cadover, the Wiltshire estate of Mrs Failing, Rickie's eccentric aunt on his father's side. Rickie and Agnes, prior to their marriage, make a visit there which ends badly. Mrs Failing has a boorish young retainer called Stephen Wonham who is neither sophisticated nor conventional. In a mischievous moment while out walking in the Cadbury Rings, an ancient Iron Age fortification, Mrs Failing tells Rickie that Stephen is his illegitimate half-brother. Rickie faints, is revived by Stephen, but is prevented from telling him of their relationship by Agnes. It is agreed that the affair be covered up and Stephen kept in ignorance.

In order to marry, Rickie gives up trying to write imaginative stories and begins work as a teacher at Sawston School. Herbert is now house master of Dunwood House and Agnes is to act as his housekeeper. Rickie soon becomes entangled in school politics and, dominated by the Pembrokes, grows increasingly unhappy. There is a scandal over the maltreatment of one of the boys and Agnes gives birth to a deformed daughter who quickly dies. Matters are brought to a head by the arrival of Stephen, now an outcast and seeking his brother. The Pembrokes try to buy him off but Ansell intervenes, telling Rickie that Stephen is his mother's son, not his father's as he 'had always supposed. Rickie collapses and shortly afterwards leaves Sawston with Stephen to begin a new life.

But Rickie's life is doomed. On a visit to Cadover he becomes disillusioned with his brother's drinking and dies saving him from an oncoming train. The novel ends some time later with Stephen now married and a reformed character. On an idyllic summer evening, before going out to sleep on the downs with his young daughter, we learn that Rickie's writings live on to give him some posthumous recognition.

What can this account tell us? Well, I found it difficult to write the story down in this way – there's much that seems important that I've been forced to leave out – and so it has made me aware how complicated it is. There's no doubt that this is a messy and sprawling tale with none of the elegant balances and formal symmetries of the Italian novels. If the novel has a shape, it seems to be the loose and episodic one of Rickie's life. My first impression, then, is that this is the pattern of an 'education' novel; that is to say Rickie Elliot is the hero, and the substance of the fiction is his struggle to grow up, discover who he is, and take control of his own destiny. This is a common form of novel from the Romantic period onwards and invariably involves the author in some examination and assessment of his or her own life. Rickie isn't Forster but there are some suggestive parallels. Forster never knew his father but both he and his hero share a lonely childhood exclusively with a much loved mother. We know enough about Forster's life to say that both are sensitive and artistic, both labour under a sense of inadequacy, and both are unhappy at school but find friendship and fulfilment at Cambridge. There the parallels between the two lives end, for Rickie's is short and rather a failure while his creator's was long and his achievements substantial, but there is enough similarity to explain why Forster writes with such power, seems less in control of the material and yet has such obvious affection for this novel.

My other first impressions are that the subject of this novel seems to be Rickie's quest for some sort of meaning to his life, a search that is ultimately thwarted, so it is a sad, even tragic tale. Taking a hint from the title, Rickie's story is a moral 'journey' where he has to choose between contending forces that seem to be symbolised by contrasting landscapes or environments. I don't think that I can go any further at this stage but I've already got some useful leads and ways of getting into the novel. Rickie is the hero and I need to study his 'journey' more closely if I'm to get a better basic grasp of the novel.

2 Select a short passage featuring one of the main characters and try to build upon the ideas you have established so far

I've decided to look at the very first impressions of Rickie that Forster gives us in the opening chapter (page references to the novel relate to the Penguin edition, 1988).

Rickie, on whose carpet the matches were being dropped, did not like to join in the discussion. It was too difficult for him. He could not even quibble. If he spoke, he should simply make himself a fool. He preferred to listen, and to watch the tobacco-smoke stealing out past the window seat into the tranquil October air. He could see the court too, and the college cat teasing the college tortoise, and the kitchen-men with supper-trays upon their heads. Hot food for one – that must be for the geographical don, who never came in for Hall; cold food for three, apparently at half a crown a head, for someone he did not know; hot food, *à la carte* – obviously for the ladies haunting the next staircase; cold food for two, at two shillings – going to Ansell's rooms for himself and Ansell, and as it passed under the lamp he saw that it was meringues again. Then the bed-makers began to arrive, chatting to each other pleasantly, and he could hear Ansell's bed-maker say, 'Oh dang!' when she found that she had to lay Ansell's tablecloth; for there was not a breath stirring. The great elms were motionless, and seemed still in the glory of midsummer, for the darkness hid the yellow blotches on their leaves, and their outlines were still rounded against the tender sky. Those elms were Dryads – so Rickie believed or pretended, and the line between the two is subtler than we admit. At all events they were lady trees, and had for generations fooled the college statutes by their residence in the haunts of youth.
But what about the cow? He returned to her with a start for this would never do. He also would try to think the matter out. Was she there or not? The cow. There or not. He strained his eyes into the night.
Either way it was attractive. If she was there, other cows were there too. The darkness of Europe was dotted with them, and in the far East their flanks were shining in the rising sun. Great herds of them stood browsing in pastures where no

man came nor need ever come, or plashed knee-deep by the brink of impassable rivers. And this, moreover, was the view of Ansell. Yet Tilliard's view had a good deal in it. One might do worse than follow Tilliard, and suppose the cow not to be there unless oneself was there to see her. A cowless world, then, stretched round him on every side. Yet he had only to peep into a field, and click! it would at once become radiant with bovine life.

Suddenly he realized that this, again, would never do. As usual, he had missed the whole point, and was overlaying philosophy with gross and senseless details. For if the cow was not there, the world and the fields were not there either. And what would Ansell care about sunlit flanks or impassable streams? Rickie rebuked his own grovelling soul, and turned his eyes away from the night, which had led him to such absurd conclusions. (pp. 3–5)

Rickie has been listening to an earnest philosophical dispute between his best friend, Ansell, and Tilliard. The subject is one of the traditional quandaries of metaphysics. Can anything be said to exist if there is no one there to perceive it? The item used as an example is a cow in a field. Is the cow really *there* in the field – does it exist – if there is nobody there to see it? Ansell takes the objective view that it does, Tilliard the subjective view that if he isn't there to see it, it can't be said to be there at all. Rickie finds it difficult to follow the abstract nature of the discussion and drifts off into poetic speculation and whimsy. This is a long and complex passage to choose for analysis, but, placed as it is at the very onset of the narrative, it is clearly important for our understanding of Rickie, and, maybe, the novel as a whole, so I think it is worth careful examination.

I would say the passage revolves around a tension in Rickie himself: between his ability to record and appreciate external reality and his tendency to day-dream and remake the world into one of ideal poetic forms that satisfy his romantic nature.

As regards the first, we get a very accurate and memorable description of a Cambridge college in a still, fine autumn evening at the turn of the century through Rickie's eyes. Along with him, we follow the drifting tobacco smoke outside into the court where the college cat teases the college tortoise. We note with him the various meals going past underneath the window and share his shrewd predictions as to whom they are destined for: hot food, cold food, food priced and food *à la carte*, meals for the reclusive don, the ladies 'haunting the next staircase', and 'meringues again' for Ansell and himself. What we are shown in the first paragraph is a lively and speculative mind, responsive to the humblest events and democratic in its interest, the comings and goings of the servants and the mild swearing of the bedmaker. All this draws us into sympathetic appreciation of Rickie himself; we are already predisposed in his favour. In the second half of this long first paragraph we get a more poetic appreciation of the great college elms practising, as it were, a kind of deception over us. At first, their beauty is qualified by their decay but the darkness conceals their 'yellow blotches', the full foliage silhouetted against the 'tender' sky making it seem like summer still. Then the mood shifts into fancy as the elms become 'Dryads' – female wood spirits from Greek mythology who have penetrated into this exclusive male preserve, fooling the college authorities.

Rickie then calls himself back to the sterner reality of the debate going on in his room, only to drift away again into a comically excessive global vision of cows in fields on both sides of the world, benighted in England but their flanks 'shining in the rising sun' in the Far East. Grown mysterious and distant, these cows browse in pastures far from man or plash at the edge of vast rivers. Thus Rickie elaborates on Ansell's contention that 'the cow is there' (p. 3) in a playful, bravura way that is comically excessive and linguistically inventive. It is a very appealing performance and culminates in the vision of Tilliard's 'cowless world' suddenly being transfigured by the perceiver into radiant 'bovine life'. It is all the more surprising, therefore, when, in the final paragraph, Rickie falls away again into curious self-abasement: he castigates his 'grovelling soul' for failing to think philosophically, but this, I feel, is not endorsed by the reader. We are not inclined to take Rickie's own view that he is too stupid for abstract debate but rather feel that his own mode of creating and re-creating reality is every bit as intelligent as his friends' disputations as to its nature. We have been delightfully entertained by a creative mind that has given us imaginative truths more appealing, because more warmly human, than abstract philosophical truth.

I think this passage places Rickie firmly at the centre of the novel; it also suggests that a crucial theme is going to be: what is the nature of reality and how can it be recognised? Other related questions include: is Rickie capable of recognising and interpreting reality correctly? How dangerous or how admirable is his tendency to poeticize it and play games with it? We might also ask ourselves what the role of Cambridge is in all this. Does it assist Rickie or lead him into dangerous self-indulgence through its rarefied and protective environment? Clearly *The Longest Journey* is going to be a philosophical novel and Rickie and his friend Ansell illustrate two contrasting approaches to this quest for truth or reality; Rickie is emotional and poetic, Ansell seems more logical and sternly abstract as befits someone training to be a philosopher. When you know the book a bit better, you will see that the cow which is so essential to this brilliant opening is never allowed to fade away. The novel's first words 'The cow is there', become a code phrase at crucial stages in the narrative (see pp. 176 and 277) that indicates Rickie's authenticity – or lack of it.

I'd like to finish with this passage by briefly considering the role of the narrator. In a way, Rickie is a proxy novelist; he is observant and imaginative and so very close to the narrator himself. The narrator is, in a sense, implicated in Rickie's musings and it becomes very difficult to distinguish between them. This could become a major problem as the book develops because the reader becomes uncertain as to what degree he or she is supposed to judge, or sympathetically identify, with the main character. This is a notorious difficulty with 'education' novels when the main character is close to, or a kind of version of, the writer himself. The treatment is bound to be ambiguous. Consider this passage. Is Rickie's imagination viewed sympathetically or not? It seems to be the former but as the passage proceeds we grow more aware that the imagination can deceive and so become potentially corrupting. Rickie leads us into unreality but, at the same time, we enjoy his awareness, his sense of mystery and poetry in the world. Moreover, the narrator seems to do so too. Yet does he share Rickie's 'grovelling' self-abasement at the end of the passage for the frivolity of his mind – or is he poking fun at him? It is hard to say.

I think it is time to move on to the next step.

3 *Select a second passage for discussion*

'Rickie!'

She was calling from the dell. For an answer he sat down where he was, on the dust-bespattered margin. She could call as loud as she liked. The devil had done much, but he should not take him to her.

'Rickie!' – and it came with the tones of an angel. He drove his fingers into his ears, and invoked the name of Gerald. But there was no sign, neither angry motion in the air nor hint of January mist. June – fields of June, sky of June, songs of June. Grass of June beneath him, grass of June over the tragedy he had deemed immortal. A bird called out of the dell: 'Rickie!'

A bird flew into the dell.

*   *   *

'Did you take me for the Dryad?' she asked. She was sitting down with his head on her lap. He had laid it there for a moment before he went out to die, and she had not let him take it away.

'I prayed you might not be a woman,' he whispered.

'Darling, I am very much a woman. I do not vanish into groves and trees. I thought you would never come to me.'

'Did you expect – ?'

'I hoped. I called hoping.'

Inside the dell it was neither June nor January. The chalk walls barred out the seasons, and the fir trees did not seem to feel their passage. Only from time to time the odours of summer slipped in from the wood above, to comment on the waxing year. She bent down to touch him with her lips.

He started, and cried passionately, 'Never forget that your greatest thing is over. I have forgotten: I am too weak. You shall never forget. What I said to you then is greater than what I say to you now. What he gave you then is greater than anything you will get from me.'

She was frightened. Again she had the sense of something abnormal. Then she said, 'What is all this nonsense?' and folded him in her arms. (pp. 73–4)

This passage is taken from the end of Chapter 7. By now, Rickie is in love with Agnes. She comes to visit him at Cambridge and goes walking with him unchaperoned. He talks about his writing and how in one of his stories a girl turns into a dryad. The tale is set in a dell full of trees, one very similar to his favourite spot, an old disused chalk pit near Madingley that is one of the 'holy places' of his imagination. As it is near where they are walking, Agnes asks to see it. Rickie feels it to be 'enchanted' and dares not enter it with her. Agnes goes in alone and calls to Rickie three times. Finally he does enter and, in a highly emotional and imaginative state, finds himself in her arms. He seems to have declared his love and been accepted.

Again, I think the tension in the passage is in Rickie himself; superficially it is between the two of them but, as in the first passage, the real conflict is between Rickie's imagination, his need to create poetic situations out of life, and the demands that the real world makes on him.

The presence of Gerald, Agnes's dead fiancé, looms heavily over this passage and to appreciate its full significance you need to look again at Rickie's reaction to seeing them both together in Chapter 3 (pp. 39–40). Rickie feels unworthy of Agnes and is reluctant to commit himself; he wishes to remain outside the dell on its 'dust-bespattered margin'. His feelings are ambiguous: on the one hand he feels tempted by the devil, for memories of Gerald haunt him; he stops his ears against Agnes's calls and expects some sort of ominous wintry warning from the past. But it doesn't come; instead he becomes overwhelmed by the lyricism of the present moment expressed in the incantatory repetition of the word 'June'. Earlier in their conversation, he had told Agnes that he wanted to 'get in touch with Nature'. Now he achieves his dearest wish and becomes a bird answering a bird.

The meeting of the lovers is placed in a lacuna, a silent gap, and when we see them again Agnes is in a dominant maternal role: Rickie has his head in her lap like a frightened child. Their first exchange reveals a conflict. Oddly Rickie has prayed that she 'might not be a woman', surely the strangest sentiment from an aspiring lover; as Agnes rightly retorts, she is 'very much a woman', not a dryad given to vanishing 'into groves and trees', though the dell itself is still seen as a place temporarily out of time and time's demands – a magic space beyond the seasons: inside, it is 'neither June nor January' with only the slightest reminders of summer to 'comment on the waxing year'. Agnes is also right about her kiss; Rickie's reaction is, by any standards, 'abnormal'; it shows both his neurotic feelings of inadequacy and an extraordinary sincerity as he tries, even in triumph, to express his sense of failure in the conventional lover's role. Whether it be his physical deformity or some deeper reason, he must express his knowledge that Gerald could fulfil Agnes in ways that he can't. Agnes, more practical and less self-critical or imaginative, gives the obvious response that is to mark the nature of their relationship hereafter. Dominant and maternal, she soothes Rickie like a frightened child. But she is right to be alarmed. This is not at all a happy, joyous engagement scene; it is full of minatory warnings and ominous signs.

I've chosen this passage because I feel it is a crucial one in deciding the direction of Rickie's development. It leads him away from Cambridge and his undergraduate friends and into Sawston and marriage. Agnes now becomes his exclusive companion in the 'longest journey' of the title. Clearly the roles of conventional courtship have been reversed. Agnes is the active, dominant one, even the seducer, while Rickie is a passive dreamer. If we think about the first passage again, I think we can see that there is a significant parallel here – a sense of repetition with variation that Forster himself thought an indispensable tool of the novelist and called 'rhythm'.

In the first passage we saw Rickie dreaming in the protective comfort of his undergraduate rooms. Soon Agnes is to burst in without ceremony and puts his friends to flight. Something similar is happening here; Forster seems to be setting up a 'rhythm' of imaginative male privacy and practical female invasion. Agnes invades Rickie's 'sacred space', the private world of his imagination, invites him in and captures him there. The writing emphasises some serious doubts as to whether Rickie can see Agnes for what she is, not a 'dryad' but a flesh and blood woman seeking a husband. Forster also seems to suggest some more sinister psychological dependency between the pair. As we've noted, the haunting presence of Gerald, the dead virile lover that Rickie can never be, hangs heavily over the passage. Rickie's preoccupation with him and his voyeuristic memory of the lovers' erotic embrace does make his own relationship with Agnes abnormal from the start. It's as if by embracing Agnes, he is embracing the feared yet desired Gerald by proxy, as well as supplanting him. We might remember, too, Agnes's own excitement at the thought of Gerald bullying Rickie (p. 50). So what evolves as a perverted pattern of female dominance and over-protection in their relationship is already implicit here.

The passage also develops what might be termed the 'cow' debate on the nature of reality. After seeing Agnes, Ansell declares that phenomena either have a real existence like the cow or are 'the subjective product of a diseased imagination ... which, to our destruction, we invest with the semblance of reality' (p. 17). The suggestion is that Rickie's Agnes is not the real one, but an over-idealised phantom of his imagination who will lead him to destruction.

Finally, we have the same implication of the narrator in Rickie's feelings that I noted in the first passage, and so the same ambiguity of judgement. The narrator empathises with Rickie's vision of being a bird flying to join a bird, sharing his excited lyricism; but, as we have seen, there are other indications that he is also standing back in judgement. He seems to share, and invite the reader to share, Agnes's view that Rickie is rather weak and 'abnormal', that his highly-strung imaginative scruples are 'un-manly'. Such ambivalence in viewpoint seems to come from Forster himself; it could become a source of moral and artistic confusion. I'm going to move on now to what is one of the high points, perhaps even the climax, of the novel.

4   Select a third passage for discussion

They approached the central tree.

'How you do puzzle me,' he said, dropping her arm and beginning to laugh. 'How could I have a half-brother?'

She made no answer.

Then a horror leapt straight at him, and he beat it back and said, 'I will not be frightened.' The tree in the centre revolved, the tree disappeared, and he saw a room – the room where his father had lived in town. 'Gently,' he told himself, 'gently.'

Still laughing, he said, 'I, with a brother – younger – it's not possible.' The horror leapt again, and he exclaimed, 'It's a foul lie!'

'My dear, my dear!'

'It's a foul lie! He wasn't – I won't stand –'

'My dear, before you say several noble things remember that it's worse for him than for you – worse for your brother, for your half-brother, for your younger brother.'

But he heard her no longer. He was gazing at the past, which he had praised so recently, which gaped ever wider, like an unhallowed grave. Turn where he would, it encircled him. It took visible form: it was this double entrenchment of the Rings. His mouth went cold, and he knew that he was going to faint among the dead. He started running, missed the exit, stumbled on the inner barrier, fell into darkness –

'Get his head down,' said a voice. 'Get the blood back into him. That's all he wants. Leave him to me. Elliot!' – the blood was returning – 'Elliot, wake up!'

He woke up. The earth he had dreaded lay close to his eyes, and seemed beautiful. He saw the structure of the clods. A tiny beetle swung on a grass blade. On his own neck a human hand pressed, guiding the blood back to his brain.

There broke from him a cry, not of horror but of acceptance. For one short moment he understood. 'Stephen – ' he began, and then he heard his own name called: 'Rickie! Rickie!' Agnes had hurried from her post on the margin, and, as if understanding also, caught him to her breast.

Stephen offered to help them further, but finding that he made things worse, he stepped aside to let them pass and then sauntered inwards. The whole field, with its concentric circles, was visible, and the broad leaves of the turnips rustled in the gathering wind. Miss Pembroke and Elliot were moving towards the Cadover entrance. Mrs Failing stood watching in her turn on the opposite bank. He was not an inquisitive boy; but as he leant against the tree he wondered what it was all about, and whether he would ever know. (pp. 130–1)

Walking in the Cadbury Rings, Mrs Failing has just told Rickie that Stephen is his illegitimate half-brother. The shock makes him faint; Stephen revives him but Agnes prevents any discussion between them. The tension here seems to be between the truth, told by Mrs Failing and exemplified by the physical presence of Stephen himself, and Rickie's resistance to the truth.

I find this a powerful piece of writing. Forster captures well the rhythm of dawning realisation in Rickie as he walks towards the central tree which becomes a symbol of the truth. (Stephen leans against it at the end of the passage.) The horror leaps, is beaten back and leaps again as Rickie fights for mental and

emotional equilibrium, the present scene shredding in his consciousness to reveal the possible significance in repressed
memories of his father's London rooms. The laughter of disbe-
lief masks fear, soon turning to anger – 'It's a foul lie!' – before
the oppression of the past overwhelms him 'like an unhallowed
grave'. This sudden sense of the overbearing weight of the past
takes visible form in the encircling 'double entrenchment' of the
Rings; their claustrophobia, the feelings of entrapment they
evoke, lead finally to panic and unconsciousness.

Stephen's intervention seems to work at both a realistic and
symbolic level. He revives Rickie physically by bringing him
blood to his head but there's a suggestion that he revives him
metaphysically, too, by bringing him to a sense of reality
through intimate contact with the earth – that physical, warm-
blooded reality of life that Rickie always seeks to avoid. As
Stephen holds him, guiding the blood back into his brain, we get
close-ups in microscopic detail of the structure of earth-clods,
the swinging beetle on the grass blade, that become beautiful
rather than to be feared. Thus Rickie is brought to a moment of
truth, a cry of acceptance and acknowledgement – 'Stephen' –
that is quickly frustrated by Agnes's intervention. Her own
repeated call of his name and her maternal embrace shielding
him from Stephen remind us, of course, of the earlier episode in
the dell which we have just discussed. Once again, we suspect
that she is not acting in Rickie's best interest by obstructing his
struggle to reach out for the truth.

As you get to know the novel better, you will come to see that
this episode is a crucial moral test for Rickie. From this failed
moment of recognition, he goes downhill rapidly; he becomes
more and more a creature of the Pembrokes and subject to
Sawston convention. It also illustrates Forster's extraordinary
topographical imagination, his feeling for landscape and the
way landscapes are shaped and given significance by history. I
think that you will also come to realise that the Rings are the
most important symbol in the novel. Created by labour and
sacrifice and hallowed by their immense age, they are the
supreme space for truth-telling. They are a place of fear and
dread – dead soldiers lie beneath the rustling turnip leaves – but

they also provide a pledge of continuity and hope. These same soldiers, we are told earlier, are said to be guarding a fabulous hoard of gold. As we have seen, Rickie is sensitive to landscape and makes his own sacred spaces, but the Rings transcend any of these and are untameable. Profoundly pagan and beyond all convention, they find out and expose his weaknesses.

We are told that the locals, punning on the associations of 'Cadbury', call the place the 'cocoa squares' (p. 97), so linking them to Ansell's obsessive and regressive doodling with circles and squares that represents his ceaseless search for the truth at the end of Chapter 1 (p. 17). Here Stephen, standing at the centre of the Rings, represents a truth for Rickie that must be faced if he is to grow as a person and get hold of his life. It is perhaps a little difficult for us to understand the stigma of illegitimacy now, but for middle-class Edwardians, it was considerable. Panic, convention and Agnes intervene to take Rickie away from the mysteries of blood brotherhood and the earth. Although there is a promise at the end of the novel that Rickie and Stephen will meet once more in the Rings, it is not fulfilled: Rickie will never enter them again.

I think the style of the passage shows how richly Forster can respond to the pagan and prehistorical as well as to the sophisticated and modern. It also contains that curious blend of psychological realism and symbolic action as Rickie walks towards the truth at the centre of the circles that is the mark of Forster's writing at its best. Rickie's gathering realisation is handled well; it is tense, dramatic and plausible and experienced from his point of view. The second half of the passage is marked by more sudden shifts of perspective as we move into a set of exterior actions. The spectacle of Stephen forcing blood (physical and emotional consciousness?) into Rickie's head, Agnes's intervention and Stephen's banishment is expressed as a kind of significant tableau. There's a scene rather reminiscent of this much later, when Stephen has a fight with Ansell in the garden of Dunwood House (pp. 208–10), though the result of this struggle is to make the two firm friends.

I want to move on now to look at a passage where Rickie is confronted by Stephen more directly near the end of the book.

5   *Select a fourth passage for discussion*

Agnes, who had not been seeing to the breakfast, chose this
moment to call from the passage. 'Of course he can't stop,' she
exclaimed. 'For better or worse, it's settled. We've none of us
altered since last Sunday week.'

'There you're right, Mrs Elliot!' he shouted, starting out of
the temperate past. 'We haven't altered.' With a rare flash of
insight he turned on Rickie. 'I see your game. You don't care
about *me* drinking, or to shake *my* hand. It's some one else you
want to cure – as it were, that old photograph. You talk to me,
but all the time you look at the photograph.' He snatched it
up. 'I've my own idea of good manners, and to look friends
between the eyes is one of them; and this' – he tore the
photograph across – 'and this' – he tore it again – 'and these – '
He flung the pieces at the man, who had sunk into a chair.
'For my part, I'm off.'

Then Rickie was heroic no longer. Turning round in his
chair, he covered his face. The man was right. He did not love
him, even as he had never hated him. In either passion he had
degraded him to be a symbol for the vanished past. The man
was right, and would have been lovable. He longed to be back
riding over those windy fields, to be back in those mystic
circles, beneath pure sky. Then they could have watched and
helped and taught each other, until the word was a reality,
and the past not a torn photograph, but Demeter the goddess
rejoicing in the spring. Ah, if he had seized those high
opportunities! For they led to the highest of all, the symbolic
moment, which, if a man accepts, he has accepted life.
(pp. 255–6)

By this stage in the novel, Rickie has spent two unhappy years as
a husband and a teacher. Stephen has now discovered the truth
of his birth, and this passage is taken from the aftermath of his
drunken return to Sawston as he seeks revenge for his rejection
by Rickie. The latter is full of remorse and attempts to make
Stephen stay so he can reform him. This plan is resisted by
Agnes, fighting for convention and respectability, and also
resented by Stephen who intuits Rickie's sentimental wish to
turn him into an image of their mother reborn, a wish symbolised in the photograph of her that he tears up.

I think we can see here the same conflict that we have noted before between Rickie's desire for consoling poetic falsities and the hard realities that must be faced.

Rickie is caught between his brother and his wife. They both reject his plans but for rather different reasons. Agnes is negative and conventional, Stephen's response is violent and without social pretence, but they both insist on a truth that Rickie seeks to evade, namely that whatever the facts of Stephen's parentage, nothing in the basic situation has changed. Stephen's tearing up of the photograph is a destructive act but also a liberating one; it's the rejection of a dead past that he never knew and that holds Rickie back. The angry and dramatic truth-telling that follows is part of Stephen's function and transcends habitual notions of good behaviour.

The second part of the passage focuses on Rickie's interior consciousness and the crucial moment of realisation that Stephen's action has brought about. After the direct social conflict of the previous paragraph, this is a compressed and complicated piece of writing traversing past memories and present regrets. Rickie seems finally to have understood the falsity of his nostalgia and how it has created fake emotions. Up till now, Stephen has not been hated or loved but merely 'a symbol for the vanished past'. The ride with Stephen on his engagement visit, which before, had seemed such a fiasco, is now seen as a glorious lost opportunity for life and comradeship. Rickie is filled with sadness for lost opportunities and desires a bolder, more fulfilling life outside convention and closer to nature – a life away from the dead past which, like the photograph, is faded and static, but more in the spirit of Demeter, the Greek goddess of the earth. Unlike the photograph, this ancient deity is always vital, always renewable. The word which would have become a reality is, of course, love; Rickie has come to see that in order to live to one's full capacity one has to be brave, take risks, seize 'the symbolic moment'.

I think the reader has the right to be a little sceptical of Rickie's 'conversion' at this point. Hasn't he merely stripped away one illusion only to replace it with another? The ride with Stephen, seen so negatively before, is now almost too lyrically re-created with the pair watching, helping and teaching each other back in the Rings, beaneath a 'pure' sky. From being a symbol of a discredited, vanished past, Stephen has been suddenly elevated into a symbol of bright, lost opportunities. Rickie's endemic facility for nostalgic poeticising is still intact. Even as he prepares to leave Sawston, this passage reveals his incorrigible tendency to idealise, first his mother, then Agnes – and now Stephen. Rickie's imagination, though often noble, still works in extremes and hinders self-knowledge. It will ultimately destroy him.

Before we leave this passage, I would like to spend a little more time considering the photograph and the idea of Demeter that Rickie places in opposition to it in the last paragraph: 'and the past not a torn photograph, but Demeter the goddess rejoicing in the spring.' It's a good opportunity to examine the way Forster weaves motifs and images into his on-going narrative that accumulate meaning in an incremental way. Both photograph and goddess are associated with Rickie's dead mother. The photograph, most obviously, is first described 'looking rather sweet' in Rickie's room at Cambridge (p. 8); the use of Demeter is more complex and richly suggestive. She is associated with the mother figure not as an individual but as an image of the life-force, fertility and hope for the future. She first appears as a picture of the Cnidian Demeter swinging from the rafters in Stephen's attic room in Cadover House; rather like Stephen himself, she is banished from Mrs Failing's polite drawing room and swings from the rafters 'like a joint of meat' (p. 118).

Later, hearing that Rickie is to be a father, Ansell regards the original statue in the British Museum and sees in her 'powers he could not cope with, nor, as yet, understand' (p. 182). Rickie's attachment to the photograph, a fading superficial resemblance, shows how nostalgically he is tied to an unfruitful image of the past; his sterility is emphasised by the death of his crippled child. The powers of Demeter are Stephen's by right; he is associated with her living force as earth mother by virtue of being a love child. Forster seems to indicate by this careful symbolic pattern-ing and cross-referencing that, while Rickie, the product of an over-cultivated, unloving father, is doomed, Stephen is the living embodiment of fruitful regeneration.

Rickie is divided between sentimental worship of his mother and hatred of his father. His feelings for Stephen are similarly extreme. When he was his father's child he was hated; now, in this passage, he is adored. Stephen rightly resents this and insists that he be accepted as he *is*. As we have seen, this is something that Rickie finds impossible to do. But the end of the novel will show that Rickie is not given over to the effete and over-cultivated influence of his father entirely; he can finally reach his mother through another aspect of Demeter. Because she lost her daughter Persephone, the goddess is also an image of grief and suffering. In his final self-sacrifice and mutilation, Rickie is associated with this aspect of her divinity. Forster underlines the kinship in the nature of the railway accident that ends his life. Rickie's death leaves him shattered at the knees like the broken statue in the British Museum.

I think I've got as much as I can out of this passage. Having looked at four passages that deal with Rickie's progress through the novel, it's time to assess the progress that we've made so far.

6   *Have I achieved a sufficiently complex sense of the novel?*

I must confess that I still find this a puzzling novel, and some, though not all, of my difficulties continue to revolve around the treatment of Rickie himself. In many ways my basic analysis has revealed an attractive hero; he is kind, imaginative and desperately wants to be good and useful in the world. True, he has weaknesses, in particular, a tendency towards moral cowardice, self-pity and a need to over-idealise people, as we have seen, but they don't seem sufficient grounds for the cruel treatment Forster deals out at the end of the novel. This is a tale of wasted potential, of defeat wrested from the jaws of victory, for it seems strange that, having found the courage to leave Sawston, Rickie still comes unstuck at the end. Indeed, the conclusion gives me a lot of problems generally; it's as if Forster suddenly loses interest in Rickie as a hero and transfers his allegiance to Stephen. Stephen's dramatic and implausible reformation doesn't seem to 'fit' the rest of the story at all; it seems to belong to a different sort of book. At the very least, I don't think we feel that Stephen has struggled enough, or realistically enough, to earn his position of pre-eminence at the end; the author's moral approval seems sentimental and biased. He seems guilty of that very same need to over-idealise certain characters that he has punished Rickie for. Certainly we shall have to examine Stephen's role in the novel, particularly in the conclusion, and try to make some sense of it.

I'm beginning to feel that this problem of inconsistent literary treatment extends to the book as a whole. Compare the Cambridge scene in the first passage with the Wiltshire one in the third. One is full of sharp, 'realistic' details of its time and place, the other seems more mysterious and timeless. Part of the difficulty with this novel is the manner in which Forster writes differently at different points in the narrative; he seems to be uncertain what he is doing. Such marked variations of style make the book unsettling, even confusing to read, and I should like to explore this aspect of the novel a little further. The question of the novel's structure may be related to this inconsistency of style. The basic shape, as we noted earlier, is the story of a man's life, but it is also divided into three sections: 'Cambridge', 'Sawston', and 'Wiltshire'. It would seem that Forster is attempting to give some additional significance and order to the narrative by imposing these three topographical sections onto Rickie's 'journey'; as each provides Rickie with its own distinctive challenges and tests, I need to try and understand what Forster means by them a little better.

Finally, there are many interesting characters in the book apart from Rickie and Stephen. I won't be able to look at them all but an examination of one or two of them will all help build up a fuller picture of the novel as a whole. My basic analysis has got me well into the narrative and helped me articulate some of the difficulties, but I still feel the need to explore further and try to make better sense of its complexities.

II Aspects of the novel

I haven't discussed Rickie's life in Sawston very much, so I'm going to start by taking a look at Herbert Pembroke, whose life revolves around Sawston School.

> Here Mr Pembroke passed his happy and industrious life. His technical position was that of master to a form low down on the Modern Side. But his work lay elsewhere. He organized. If no organization existed, he would create one. If one

did exist, he would modify it. 'An organization,' he would say, 'is after all not an end in itself. It must contribute to a movement.' When one good custom seemed likely to corrupt the school, he was ready with another; he believed that without innumerable customs there was no safety, either for boys or men. Perhaps he is right, and always will be right. Perhaps each of us would go to ruin if for one short hour we acted as we thought fit, and attempted the service of perfect freedom. The school caps, with their elaborate symbolism, were his; his the many-tinted bathing-drawers, that showed how far a boy could swim; his the hierarchy of jerseys and blazers. It was he who instituted Bounds, and Call, and the two sorts of exercise-paper, and the three sorts of caning, and 'The Sawstonian', a bi-terminal magazine. His plump finger was in every pie. The dome of his skull, mild but impressive, shone at every masters' meeting. He was generally acknowledged to be the coming man. (p. 43)

The tone of this passage is fiercely ironic. At one level we are given a picture of Herbert as a model of efficiency and industry – the 'coming man' – but there's enough here to give us the clue to the narrator's real feeling that he is an officious fool. Herbert's limited intelligence – 'master to a form low down' – is signalled without being underlined at the outset. Energy he certainly has in abundance, and this goes into an obsessive pursuit of tidiness and 'organization'. I think that this is seen as a fear and dislike of any activity suggesting spontaneity, creativity or individuality. It also shows a ruthless ambition to stamp everything in his image and an inability to leave well alone. Orders, hierarchies, regulations – they reveal the totalitarian mentality that is fearful of freedom.

How a writer achieves such an ironic tone so that the reader reads one thing but understands quite another, is never very easy to analyse; I certainly begin to pick it up here with the snatches we are given of Herbert's philosophy, his eagerness to replace a 'corrupt' good custom with another more to his liking. The narrator's disagreement with Herbert's low opinion of humanity is expressed in a complex way; his belief that we wouldn't necessarily 'go to ruin' without protecting conventions or, maybe, it would be better if we did, comes across through the use of the language of religious aspiration – 'the service of perfect freedom' – and poetic yearning – 'one short hour'. Part of the comic effect is the use of metonymy, reducing school boys to component parts in a great bureaucratic machine: caps and bathing-trunks (colour-coded), jerseys and blazers. 'Bounds' and 'Call' are again restrictions of freedom and movement. With increasing comedy, Herbert's malign influence intrudes into work – 'the two sorts of exercise-paper' – and finally, a nice bizarre touch this, 'the three sorts of caning'. One doesn't have too much confidence in the creativity and readability of 'The Sawstonian'. By the end, Herbert himself has become part of his own machine, a plump finger and a shining domed skull. At first glance, the satire seems slight and affectionate enough; Herbert is 'mild but impressive', 'happy and industrious', an amiable busy-bodying buffoon, but actually, read carefully, he becomes rather sinister. Police states are run by such people convinced of their own good motives.

The writing here is different from any previous passage that I've examined in the book. The satire goes beyond comic zest in describing an awful person to expose the corruption of a whole social system. The English public school is seen as a kind of hell. False order, 'respectable' middle-class oppression, begin here in Sawston and eventually permeate throughout all society. Think of Wilbraham, the estate-manager at Cadover, keeping the rustics in order; seeing society as a kind of map, he wishes to maintain rigid hierarchies also (p. 97). Just as Herbert oppresses his boys, so the gentry oppress the countryside through their minions.

Through Herbert, we have got the feel of 'Sawston' and the world of deadening rules and conventions that it signifies. I want to move on now and examine another kind of symbolic land-scape.

> The rain tilted a little from the south-west. For the most part it fell from a grey cloud silently, but now and then the tilt increased, and a kind of sigh passed over the country as the drops lashed the walls, trees, shepherds, and other motionless objects that stood in their slanting career. At times the cloud would descend and visibly embrace the earth, to which it had only sent messages; and the earth itself would bring forth cloud – clouds of a whiter breed – which formed in the shallow valleys and followed the courses of the streams. It

seemed the beginning of life. Again God said, 'Shall we divide the waters from the land or not? Was not the firmament labour and glory sufficient?' At all events it was the beginning of life pastoral, behind which imagination cannot travel.

Yet complicated people were getting wet – not only the shepherds. For instance, the piano-tuner was sopping. So was the vicar's wife. So were the lieutenant and the peevish damsels in his Battlesden car. Gallantry, charity, and art pursued their various missions, perspiring and muddy, while out on the slopes beyond them stood the eternal man and the eternal dog, guarding eternal sheep until the world is vegetarian.

Inside the arbour – which faced east, and thus avoided the bad weather – there sat a complicated person who was dry. She looked at the drenched world with a pleased expression, and would smile when a cloud lay down on the village, or when the rain sighed louder than usual against her solid shelter. Ink, paper-clips, and foolscap paper were on a table before her, and she could also reach an umbrella, a waterproof, a walking stick, and an electric bell. Her age was between elderly and old, and her forehead was wrinkled with an expression of slight but perpetual pain. But the lines round her mouth indicated that she had laughed a great deal during her life, just as the clean tight skin round her eyes perhaps indicated that she had not often cried. She was dressed in brown silk. A brown silk shawl lay most becomingly over her beautiful hair. (pp. 85–6)

In these opening paragraphs to Chapter 10, we are introduced to 'Wiltshire' and Mrs Failing, owner of Cadover House. I find this strange, complex and artful writing. It differs from the previous passage because, presumably, Forster is trying to do different things here. Initially, it describes a rain-drenched countryside not straightforwardly, but in a highly mediated and playful manner. The narrator is linguistically and imaginatively fanciful, much as Rickie was with the cow in the first passage we looked at. The Wiltshire landscape is described in terms of the creation of the world in the opening of Genesis. Such writing we can term 'mythopoetic' because it uses poetry and myth instead of simple, direct observation. It is so wet that we seem again to be in primal chaos before the waters were divided from the dry

land; 'It seemed the beginning of life' and God is still debating
with Himself as to whether He should proceed with His labour
and create heaven and earth from the firmament.

The landscape is pantheistically animated: earth and water
are in a reciprocal relationship – they 'visibly embrace' – and the
first paragraph is marked by the use of personification. The rain
sighs and lashes, clouds 'descend', and the earth brings forth its
own white mists. In this 'beginning of life', shepherds (we learn
later that Stephen is one featured here) lose their human
identity and become part of the landscape like walls, trees and
other 'motionless objects'.

Civilisation enters in the second paragraph with the complication of class and status, but the rain is no respecter of persons –
the piano-tuner, the vicar's wife, the lieutenant and his companions all get wet; the defences of the 'Battlesden car' prove
powerless against the weather. Forster's use of personification
becomes more ironic with the sight of 'Gallantry', 'charity' and
'art' perspiring and muddy. The clash of abstract and concrete
exposes the superficiality of these people and their concerns
when placed in the enduring perspective of the earth and its
labour: 'the eternal man and the eternal dog, guarding the
eternal sheep'. These primal figures seem to work in quite a
different time-scale, have a heroic, enduring dignity compared
with the petty irritations of the 'peevish damsels'. Contemporary
society girls are really as dated as the language that describes
them, while the shepherd and his dog will exist until all human
and animal life is extinct.

The third paragraph introduces Mrs Failing, 'a complicated
person who was dry'. From her superior vantage point with all
its creature comforts and conveniences – umbrella, water-proof,
walking-stick – and all the apparatus of culture and literacy –
ink, paper-clips, foolscap – she rejoices in her triumph over
nature, and the misfortunes of those below. In her weather-
proof 'arbour' she plays at being close to nature but ensures she
is discreetly set apart from it. Enigmatic, well-preserved and
tastefully dressed, she is certainly civilised but also heartless,
'failing' to connect with strong emotions as her name suggests.

We can compare this passage with the previous one and ask
ourselves what part does such a character set in such a landscape
play in the overall design of the text? Mrs Failing is akin to
Herbert in that both seek to control and manipulate others, but

she seems a more enigmatic figure and is portrayed with greater subtlety. The novel sets out to show that both are a danger to Rickie and seek to lure him into false ways of life, but the satirical force in the first passage lies in the way Herbert is made to typify a whole set of bad values; 'Sawston' and its dreadful school seems to stand for all that is wrong in modern society and Herbert is identified with his background. This would not be true of Mrs Failing here. The effect of the writing, as we have seen, is to ensure that we experience 'Wiltshire' as a poetic, mysterious, and primeval place that has an independent existence apart from the social lives of those that happen to live there. Mrs Failing, as the passage shows, is denied – or denies herself – the magical potency that the narrator finds in the landscape. She serves to illustrate, in a very obvious way, Rickie's similar tendency to retreat from life and the energies of nature for the comforts of a private over-cultivated world. He shares the 'failing' of his father's family in this respect.

To return to the problem of the three sections. If the mental and cultural freedom of 'Cambridge' seems to be Ansell's domain and Herbert rules supreme in 'Sawston', it is the 'eternal shepherd' that belongs here and that, of course, turns out to be Stephen. Part of the oddness of his portrayal in the novel is because of this mysterious link he has with nature. He doesn't have a social identity as the other characters do, but seems to be just 'right' by instinct. He functions as a moral touchstone; other characters are judged to be good or bad by the way they respond to him. I want to examine his curiously privileged role in more detail by looking at that point in the novel when he and Rickie are at their closest.

Meanwhile Stephen called from the water for matches: there was some trick with paper which Mr Failing had shown him, and which he would show Rickie now, instead of talking nonsense. Bending down, he illuminated the dimpled surface of the ford. 'Quite a current,' he said, and his face flickered out of the darkness. 'Yes, give me the loose paper, quick! Crumple it into a ball.'

Rickie obeyed, though intent on the transfigured face. He believed that a new spirit dwelt there, expelling the crudities of youth. He saw steadier eyes, and the sign of manhood set like a bar of gold upon steadier lips. Some faces are knit by beauty, or by intellect, or by a great passion: had Stephen's waited for the touch of the years?

But they played as boys who continued the nonsense of the railway carriage. The paper caught fire from the match, and spread into a rose of flame. 'Now gently with me,' said Stephen, and they laid it flower-like on the stream. Gravel and tremulous weeds leapt into sight, and then the flower sailed into deep water, and up leapt the two arches of the bridge. 'It'll strike!' they cried; 'No, it won't; it's chosen the left,' and one arch became a fairy tunnel, dropping diamonds. Then it vanished for Rickie; but Stephen, who knelt in the water, declared that it was still afloat, far through the arch, burning as if it would burn for ever. (pp. 272–3)

In terms of the plot, this is a minor episode but, as so often in Forster, the writing suggests otherwise. Two grown men playing a silly game with paper fire-boats hardly seems matter for the climax of a complicated novel but, even with a slight knowledge of the book, I think we register that this is an important and significant moment. Remember that it occurs on the brothers' last journey to Cadover; soon Rickie will despair of reforming Stephen but die saving him from an oncoming train. Even in his disillusion, Rickie sacrifices himself that Stephen may live. This may seem psychologically implausible but a passage like this helps us understand why, for Forster, this is the necessary and satisfactory conclusion to his novel.

What the passage reveals is Forster's almost mystical belief in the strength of male brotherhood and the power that it has to preserve, sustain and continue certain values and beliefs from the past through the present and into the future. (Remember that the book's dedication is 'fratribus' which means 'to the brothers'.) Forster is not unambiguously straightforward in explaining what these values might be, but they seem to have something to do with fertility of the imagination, cultural freedom and procreative powers that transcend the making of children; it's not easy to be more specific than this. These values are not best sustained through conventional heterosexual relationships and I think we can pick up Forster's hostility to marriage – the traditional mode of social continuity – throughout the text. It is underlined by the use of the Shelley quotation that forms the basis for the novel's title. There is something pagan, earthy and pre-industrial about these values, as there is about Stephen, who, of course, is increasingly seen to embody them. So what Forster seems to be signalling in this passage is a mystical transference of power and authority from Rickie to Stephen who is to become the new hero. Rickie's sacrifice will prepare the way for new, visionary possibilities.

This is a difficult set of ideas to get across to the reader and Forster uses his most suggestive and poetic mode of writing here. Part of the effect is achieved through the use of elemental imagery and the way in which earth, air, fire and water all seem to be working towards some mutual illumination and harmony. We often think of life as a river and running water features predominantly in the narrative to suggest the instability and fleeting nature of human life as well as the flow and continuity of human history, but the river here can be crossed by ford and bridge which also suggests reconciliation and connections across time. Similarly Mrs Failing's 'trick' can be taken symbolically as a message of hope passed on from the past to future generations. Paper crumpled into a ball reminds me of Ansell's quest for truth through squares within circles, now finally fused into a 'rose of flame'. Floating 'flower-like' on the stream, the flame is illusive, transient and vulnerable, but briefly transforms the humble reality of weeds, gravel and arch into miraculous beauty.

Stephen's face, flickering out of the darkness, is also 'trans-figured' by the flame; eyes and lips are highlighted to anticipate Stephen's transformation from rough primitive yokel into the spiritual inheritor purged of 'the crudities of youth'. The fanciful nature of Rickie's imagination, which sometimes gets criticised by Forster, seems to find a measure of support here. I think we can read the use of the two arches as similarly prophetic; the flame travels through one leaving the other unlit. Its progress through the left-hand one is then watched by the kneeling Stephen, but it is invisible to Rickie. This suggests that Stephen's line through his mother will 'burn for ever' while Rickie's is doomed to extinction.

I think we are now getting into a better position to understand the difficulties Forster had with this novel. Its materials and message were very personal and important to him, but difficult to express in the conventional format of heterosexual fiction where they become 'unrealistic'. As he wrote later in an intro-duction to the novel, he sometimes 'went wrong deliberately, as

if the spirit of anti-literature had jogged my elbow'. Part of the
unevenness of style and method I noted earlier is a tension, even
contradiction, in the text between a hostile treatment of contemporary society, full of social comment, and yearnings towards an
ideal England where true brotherhood can flourish. This other
'England' is based in the renovatory powers of the natural
landscape, is mythically conceived, and has little to do with
contemporary social life. To reconcile these two versions of
reality provides Forster with a severe test, and I should like to
conclude by examining a passage from the final chapter.

'Stevie, dear, please me more – don't take her with you.'
At this he laughed impertinently. 'I suppose I'm being kept
in line,' she called, and, though he could not see her, she
stretched her arms towards him. For a time he stood motionless, under her window, musing on his happy tangible life.
Then his breath quickened, and he wondered why he was
here, and why he should hold a warm child in his arms. 'It's
time we were starting,' he whispered, and showed the sky,
whose orange was already fading into green. 'Wish everything
good night.'
'Good night, dear mummy,' she said sleepily. 'Good night,
dear house. Good night, you pictures – long picture – stone
lady. I see you through the window – your faces are pink.'
The twilight descended. He rested his lips on her hair, and
carried her, without speaking, until he reached the open
down. He had often slept here himself alone, and on his
wedding night, and he knew that the turf was dry, and that if
you laid your face to it you would smell the thyme. For a
moment the earth aroused her, and she began to chatter. 'My
prayers – ' she said anxiously. He gave her one hand, and she
was asleep before her fingers had nestled in its palm. Their
touch made him pensive, and again he marvelled why he, the
accident, was here. He was alive and had created life. By
whose authority? Though he could not phrase it, he believed
that he guided the future of our race, and that, century after
century, his thoughts and passions would triumph in England.
The dead who had evoked him, the unborn whom he would
evoke – he governed the paths between them. By whose
authority? (pp. 288–9)

In the sudden flash-forward of these closing pages, Stephen has matured, married and settled down with his wife and child to farm near Cadover. Our final view of him is a pensive one as, having sent Herbert packing, he reflects on his good fortune. Apart from the mild eccentricity of sleeping outdoors on a warm summer's evening, it seems a conventional enough ending at first glance. Marriage, after all, is a traditional method of finishing a novel and one we've come to expect. Given that Rickie is dead, it is appropriate that his sacrifice has not been in vain. But our natural desire for a happy outcome shouldn't blind us to the oddities in the situation. Only a chapter before, Rickie had died thinking all life a 'ridiculous dream' (p. 282). It seems that Forster, weary of Rickie's troublesome and unresolvable problems, has put him away to indulge in some fairly transparent wish-fulfilment. You might argue that this ending has been anticipated in the previous flame-rose passage that we've just discussed, but isn't the reader entitled to some human, psychological plausibility as well?

These are real difficulties and your judgements will be affected by your own views on what fiction can legitimately do, and whether Forster can shift and change your assumptions. There is a case for seeing the ending as weak but there's also a case for seeing it as rather bold and provocative. Maybe for Forster, any conventional ending, happy or sad, would be untruthful and he had to write in a spirt of 'anti-literature' that conflicts with our everyday expectations. We have a marriage and a family at the end of the novel, as we might expect, but Forster's treatment of them is very unusual. . Stephen's real marriage – his real commitment – is outside the cosy domesticity of the house with the earth which he goes to like a lover – as he has before, 'alone, and on his wedding night'. The wife is a voice only, or an unseen outline with outstretched arms. She is hardly a sexual partner; Stephen seems to have drawn his fertility, the pledge of his continuance, out of the earth and – in some mysterious way – out of Rickie's death.

The demands of heterosexual marriage which destroyed Rickie are very marginal here. The wife is to be kept 'in line' and the real bonds of continuity are between men. The daughter is more symbol than flesh and blood child and, like the wife, unnamed. Part of her function is to be a visible sign that the shared inheritance of the two brothers will continue. This is the meaning of her childish babble. The two pictures coloured by the setting sun celebrate the abiding presence of their common mother in a mythical as well as an obviously physical way. The 'long picture' is the faded photograph of Stockholm where Stephen was conceived; the 'stone lady' is the Cnidian Demeter who, as we have seen, holds out the promise of fertility and continuity. Held separately by the two brothers throughout the book, they have finally come together under Stephen's roof.

So the strange mixture of the mythical and the ordinary continues to the end. It is, perhaps, unprofitable to speculate too much on Forster's own needs, but it would seem that Rickie is a troublesome *alter-ego* who contains too many of Forster's own fears and weaknesses. Because his hero was crippled in mind and body, Forster could see no future for Rickie in this world, but his own imagination was highly charged with those thoughts of male sacrifice and magical substitution that are prevalent in many ancient fertility rites. In a sense, Rickie must live on in a newly sensitised Stephen made aware of his awesome responsibilities. Stephen now governs the path between the dead and the unborn; it is he who guides 'the future of our race', and must ensure that the right values prevail. In order to reach out and affirm the need for this better future through Stephen, Forster obviously felt he must explore magical, primitive solutions to his novel that are far older than any secular, rational sense of truth or plausibility.

6
The Second English Novel: *Howards End* (1910)

I Constructing an overall analysis

Howards End is a fresh departure for Forster, and an altogether more ambitious project than any of his previous novels. An account of the plot will show this clearly.

1 *After reading the novel, think about the story and what kind of pattern you can see in the text*

The intellectual Schlegel sisters, Margaret and Helen, lead a comfortable, cultured existence in London with their younger brother Tibby. While holidaying abroad, they meet a more conventional middle-class family, the Wilcoxes, a chance event that is to have profound consequences for all their lives. The novel opens with a brief and disastrous flirtation between Helen and Paul, the youngest Wilcox son, when she visits the family home, a modest farm house called Howards End in Hertfordshire. Initially Helen is infatuated with the decisive masculine energy of the Wilcoxes but then is repulsed by their timid conventionality. The affair breaks up amid much social confusion and anger. Only Mrs Wilcox keeps her serene temper, and, despite some difficulties, she and Margaret develop a close friendship when they become temporary neighbours in London. Mrs Wilcox hears that the Schlegels are soon to lose their London home, and when she dies suddenly it transpires that she wishes to leave Howards End, which is her own inheritance, to Margaret. Margaret has no knowledge of this and Mrs Wilcox's scribbled note is ignored as illegal by the rest of her resentful family.

Two years pass and then, once more, a chance meeting brings the two families together. The sisters wish to help a struggling city clerk called Leonard Bast and when they happen to meet Henry Wilcox, the head of the family, they ask for his advice. Henry is drawn to Margaret, the more moderate and accommodating of the sisters; on the pretext of helping her find a new home, he woos her and quickly proposes marriage. Though not blind to his faults, she is attracted to him and accepts, much to the alarm and consternation of her sister. Before her own marriage, however, Margaret must help Henry organise the wedding of his daughter, Evie. This is to take place at Oniton Grange, Henry's new country house in Shropshire, for Howards End is now considered unsuitable as a home for any of the Wilcoxes and is unoccupied. The wedding at Oniton brings some unwelcome revelations. Helen arrives at the end of the celebrations in great anger, with Leonard and his wife Jacky in tow. Leonard has lost his job through Henry's bad advice and Helen demands immediate redress. It also becomes evident that Jacky has once been Henry's mistress. Margaret does her best to protect Henry by sending the Basts a dismissive note; in consequence, Helen goes abroad without seeing her sister again. Margaret forgives Henry and they marry, but the problem of finding a proper home remains unsolved as Henry no longer wishes to live at Oniton Grange. The Schlegel house is pulled down and the furniture stored at Howards End as a temporary measure. Hearing queer rumours, Margaret visits the house to discover that the furniture has been unpacked and put into place by Miss Avery, an eccentric farm woman who knew Mrs Wilcox in her youth.

Meanwhile, Helen continues to avoid her family and her behaviour begins to look increasingly odd; concerned about her state of mind, Margaret agrees reluctantly to Henry's plan of surprising her when she goes to Howards End to collect some books. To her alarm, she finds that Helen is pregnant. Helen requests to stay one night in Howards End with her sister amongst their family possessions. Henry refuses but Margaret ignores his wishes and decides to leave him and return to Germany with Helen. We learn that Helen had given herself briefly and impulsively to Leonard Bast who has been suffering guilt and remorse ever since. Events move towards a final catastrophe when he arrives at Howards End the following morning to see Margaret, is assaulted by Charles, the eldest Wilcox son, and dies of heart failure. Charles is imprisoned for manslaughter and his father breaks down. Margaret takes him, along with Helen, to recover at Howards End.

The novel ends with a family gathering some months later. Helen has given birth to a boy. Henry Wilcox gives Howards End to Margaret and Leonard's child will eventually inherit the house.

We can see from this outline of the story that *Howards End* has a much broader social sweep than any of Forster's previous novels. It seems a conventional, even old-fashioned fiction, too, with plenty of dramatic incidents like an unpopular will, shocking revelations, strange coincidences, sudden deaths, love affairs and a happy ending to keep the reader involved and entertained. If we look a little closer, it is apparent that the destiny of a house lies at the heart of this tale. This is signalled by the title, of course, but it is also made evident by the plot; the book begins and ends at Howards End, and the house makes strategic reappearances throughout the narrative. It lies at the centre of a struggle between the two families in the story, the Schlegels and the Wilcoxes, and so has some significance for Forster that an account of the plot alone cannot reveal.

A further clue on how we are to read the novel lies in the little rubric that Forster has placed on the title page: 'only connect . . .' It will be obvious from our initial reading that the Wilcoxes and the Schlegels are contrasting characters in almost every way, so I think we can assume that the project of this novel is to achieve some sort of harmony or reconciliation between these two families, and the house itself has an important role to play in this. Attitudes to the house appear important in the way we are led to assess and judge character too. The Wilcoxes own Howards End but don't seem to value it, while the Schlegel sisters lead a rootless kind of existence in London but do instinctively appreciate what the house has to offer, so their eventual possession of it has some kind of poetic justice.

Howards End isn't the only book to be named after a house; Jane Austen's *Mansfield Park* (1814) and Dickens's *Bleak House* (1853) come immediately to my mind. Austen uses her house as an emblem of certain social values that she sees as under threat, while Dickens uses his more metaphorically expansive title to suggest the poor state of a whole social system. I suspect that Forster's own title has similar ramifications. True, *Howards End* is about Howards End, but Forster's concerns extend far wider than the destiny of one particular house. Howards End – the house – is the focus, but, as we can see, Forster ranges far more widely throughout England and English society than in any of his previous novels. The shape and structure of *Howards End* is that of a 'Condition of England' novel, a form of fiction that came into prominence during the Victorian period. Such novels endeavour to engage with as much of English society as they can by means of a number of contrasts and conflicts – social, geographical, moral and political – seeking to ask some serious questions about the health of society and the future of the nation as a whole. *Howards End* is a novel of this kind.

It's time we found our way into the text and looked at it a little more closely. Forster once called the novel 'a hunt for a home': the Schlegels lose their house during the story and Margaret in particular is most concerned to find a new one. Though Helen is the more obviously attractive and dynamic of the sisters – most of the novel's main actions are precipitated through her – Margaret is clearly at the centre and the most important character. She is the 'connecter' in her friendship with Ruth Wilcox and marriage to Henry; it is to her that Howards End will eventually belong, and it is her thoughts and inner development which we follow most closely. Consequently our efforts to construct a basic analysis will best be served by examining her progress through the book.

2   *Select a short passage featuring one of the main characters and try to build upon the ideas you have established so far*

I'm going to look at a passage early in the novel where the Schlegel sisters discuss the Wilcoxes after Helen's débâcle with Paul (page references to the novel relate to the Penguin edition, 1989).

'To think that because you and a young man meet for a

moment, there must be all these telegrams and anger,' sup-
plied Margaret.

Helen nodded.

'I've often thought about it, Helen. It's one of the most
interesting things in the world. The truth is that there is a
great outer world that you and I have never touched – a life in
which telegrams and anger count. Personal relations, that we
think supreme, are not supreme there. There love means
marriage settlements, death, death duties. So far I'm clear.
But here my difficulty. This outer world, though obviously
horrid, often seems the real one – there's grit in it. It does
breed character. Do personal relations lead to sloppiness in
the end?'

'Oh, Meg, that's what I felt, only not so clearly, when the
Wilcoxes were so competent, and seemed to have their hands
on all the ropes.'

'Don't you feel it now?'

'I shall remember Paul at breakfast,' said Helen quietly. 'I
shall never forget him. He had nothing to fall back upon. I
know that personal relationships are the real life, for ever and
ever.'

'Amen!'

So the Wilcox episode fell into the background, leaving
behind it memories of sweetness and horror that mingled, and
the sisters pursued the life that Helen had commended. They
talked to each other and to other people, they filled the tall
thin house at Wickham Place with those whom they liked or
could befriend. They even attended public meetings. (p. 41)

The substance of this passage is a conversation between the
two sisters about the Wilcoxes and what they represent. They
perceive a big difference between their own belief in the value of
a rich, intimate private life and the Wilcoxes' very different
priorities. The 'great outer world' of 'telegrams and anger',
marriage settlements and death duties is contrasted with the
inner life where love and death are emotional realities. The
discussion begs the question: where does true reality lie? Is
valuing the private life a sloppy indulgence and does the outer
world provide the only substantial way to live through its
demanding discipline and 'grit'? The honest way in which the

Schlegel sisters face up to the challenge of this question must, I think, draw us to their side in the argument. Helen remembers Paul's reaction at breakfast when faced with the reality and consequences of his desires – what she calls earlier his 'panic and emptiness' (p. 41) – and how inadequate he was to face the challenge. She insists that it is intellectual and emotional self-scrutiny that provide the 'grit' and capability to put one's hands on 'all the ropes'. For her, true reality lies in personal relations 'for ever and ever', a fervent creed to which Margaret's 'Amen' finally and religiously concurs.

What we have here is the formal exposition of a conflict which the whole novel will debate and seek to resolve. We can also see that, even at this stage, there is a differentiation being made between the two sisters and a tension between their views. Helen has decided after her experiences with Paul to reject the Wilcoxes entirely. Her initial admiration has gone to the other extreme of flat hostility. Margaret is more thoughtful, more considered in her analysis. It is she who has the more acute sense of her privileged existence and a more ambiguous response to the challenges of 'the great outer world'; it is 'horrid' but often seems to be the 'real' one too. It is her questioning of where true value lies that will continue throughout the book. In the final paragraph we are shown something of the pattern of the Schlegel's daily life. The insulated world of Wickham Place with its amiable discussions and attendance at public meetings seems commendable, but also rather sterile and over-protected. The effect of this is to unsettle Helen's confident assertion and align the narrative more with Margaret's doubts. 'The Wilcox episode' with which the novel opens, bruising though it was with its 'telegrams and anger', still belongs to a different order of experience. It has left behind 'horror' but also 'sweetness'.

The passage is divided into dialogue and third person narrative, a conventional and well-tried method of telling a story. Dialogue gives dramatic immediacy, the authorial presence has the effect of distancing the action and placing it in a wider context. It gives the reader a reassuring sense of power and control; it's as if he or she were looking over the writer's shoulder – viewing the action from the same perspective as he is. The phrases that Margaret uses here – 'telegrams and anger' and 'hands on all the ropes' – occur again and again in the authorial narrative, always in slightly different or more complex contexts that enrich and complicate their meaning. Because they are used by the ʼomnipresent narrator who comments and moralises on the action, this has the effect of giving Margaret a particular authority that no other character possesses. We hear her views and share more of her intimate thoughts than anyone else's. So it is clear that we are to take Margaret as the novel's central spokesman and it is she who is voicing an important dilemma here; there are two ways and philosophies of life that appear to be irreconcilable but necessary to existence. Is it possible to connect them in some way that might mitigate the 'anger' in one and the 'sloppiness' in the other?

I think the next step forward is to look at Margaret's relationship with Ruth Wilcox.

3   Select a second passage for discussion

Mrs Wilcox was silenced. In growing discomfort they drove homewards. The city seemed Satanic, the narrower streets oppressing like the galleries of a mine. No harm was done by the fog to trade, for it lay high, and the lighted windows of the shops were thronged with customers. It was rather a darkening of the spirit which fell back upon itself, to find a more grievous darkness within. Margaret nearly spoke a dozen times, but something throttled her. She felt petty and awkward, and her meditations on Christmas grew more cynical. Peace? It may bring other gifts, but is there a single Londoner to whom Christmas is peaceful? The craving for excitement and for elaboration has ruined that blessing. Goodwill? Had she seen any example of it in the hordes of purchasers? Or in herself? She had failed to respond to this invitation merely because it was a little queer and imaginative – she, whose birthright it was to nourish imagination! Better to have accepted, to have tired themselves a little by the journey, than coldly to reply, 'Might I come some other day?' Her cynicism left her. There would be no other day. This shadowy woman would never ask her again.

They parted at the Mansions. Mrs Wilcox went in after due civilities, and Margaret watched the tall, lonely figure sweep up the hall to the lift. As the glass doors closed on it she had the sense of an imprisonment. The beautiful head disappeared first, still buried in the muff; the long trailing skirt followed. A woman of undefinable rarity was going up heavenward, like a specimen in a bottle. And into what a heaven – a vault as of hell, sooty black, from which soots descended! (pp. 94–5)

At this point in the novel, Margaret and Mrs Wilcox have gone out on a Christmas shopping expedition to the West End that ends in bad temper and failure. Mrs Wilcox has learnt, with horrified concern, that the Schlegels are to lose their family home and spontaneously invites Margaret to come and see Howards End at once. Margaret, surprised at the abruptness of the invitation and concerned about Mrs Wilcox's health, declines. As a result, the cordiality between the two rapidly deteriorates. This passage describes their uncomfortable drive home from Margaret's point of view.

The passage is dominated by a negative view of London, the 'Satanic' city, which seems to conspire with the social unease of the pair and their inability to communicate. Despite the superficial festivity of the crowds and the well-lit shops, fog and darkness prevail overall. Wealthy shopping is transformed into its opposite, an image of hard labour; the lesser streets seem 'like the galleries of a mine'. The Christmas spirit is society's most obvious attempt at connection and, for Margaret, its failure casts doubts on the validity of the inner life as well. Her darkening spirit falls back upon itself only to find 'a more grievous darkness within'. She sees the festivities as merely a craving for 'excitement and for elaboration', an expression of the underlying poverty of spirit and restlessness that is the inevitable consequence of modern city life.

In this cynical mood she begins to reflect upon herself. She also is infected. Despite her claims for, and commitment to, the inner life, she has been unable to respond to Mrs Wilcox's imaginative gesture towards her and must pay the penalty. She has betrayed her ideals, failed to 'connect' and now the moment has gone for ever. With disappointed concern and a gathering sense of pathos, she watches the 'shadowy woman' disappear into the gloomy impersonality of the Mansions, and up to her flat.

I think you will find that this is just one of a number of passages in the novel that present modern urban life as a rootless and restless existence. Unable to nourish the spirit, the modern city is profoundly inimical to personal relationships. In a book dedicated to 'connection', it shows how frail human connections are, how easily broken and destroyed. The fog is as much metaphysical as physical: it divides Margaret and Mrs Wilcox but does not interfere with trade. The city is also a jail; it imprisons its inhabitants and divides them from their best selves, as Margaret is in her cynical reflections. Our last view of Mrs Wilcox, 'buried' in her muff, is her ascension by glass lift into a sooty vault 'like a specimen in a bottle'. This is a strange image; it suggests both artificial preservation and death – a kind of life in death – in an unsympathetic, hostile environment. The final tableau mockingly evokes traditional religious imagery. The saintly Mrs Wilcox, 'a woman of undefinable rarity', is swept mechanically upwards into a horrible parody of heavenly bliss. This is the last memorable image we have of her, a sharp contrast to our first view of her trailing her long skirts over the wet lawn at Howards End, her hands full of hay (p. 36).

The mode of narration shows the blending of Margaret's thoughts with those of the narrator so that they become indistinguishable from each other in places – the judgements on London, for example. Finally, I think it is worth remembering how the movement in this passage is part of a larger 'rhythm' in the text that seems designed to show how precarious life is, how open to chance and random events. Margaret's instinct here to retreat and then reach out for Mrs Wilcox is taken up in the wider context of the chapter from which it is taken. She changes her mind, seeks out Mrs Wilcox at King's Cross, but their visit to Howards End is again frustrated by the sudden arrival of the rest of the Wilcox family. So Margaret's intuition proves correct; she will never get another invitation to the house. Soon Mrs Wilcox will be dead and Margaret will not see Howards End until after her engagement to Henry.

Let's move on now and look at a passage that shows Margaret with Henry Wilcox.

4   Select a third passage for discussion

The dining-room was big, but over-furnished. Chelsea would have moaned aloud. Mr Wilcox had eschewed those decorative schemes that wince, and relent and refrain, and achieve beauty by sacrificing comfort and pluck. After so much self-colour and self-denial, Margaret viewed with relief the sumptuous dado, the frieze, the gilded wall-paper, amid whose foliage parrots sang. It would never do with her own furniture, but those heavy chairs, that immense sideboard loaded with presentation plate, stood up against its pressure like men. The room suggested men, and Margaret, keen to derive the modern capitalist from the warriors and hunters of the past, saw it as an ancient guest-hall, where the lord sat at meat amongst his thanes. Even the Bible – the Dutch Bible that Charles had brought back from the Boer War – fell into position. Such a room admitted loot.

'Now the entrance-hall.'

The entrance-hall was paved.

'Here we fellows smoke.'

We fellows smoked in chairs of maroon leather. It was as if a motor-car had spawned. 'Oh jolly!' said Margaret, sinking into one of them.

'You do like it?' he said, fixing his eyes on her upturned face, and surely betraying an almost intimate note. 'It's all rubbish not making oneself comfortable. Isn't it?'

'Ye-es. Semi-rubbish. Are those Cruikshanks?'

'Gillrays. Shall we go on upstairs?'

'Does all the furniture come from Howards End?'

'The Howards End furniture has all gone to Oniton.'

'Does – However, I'm concerned with the house, not the furniture. How big is this smoking-room?'

'Thirty by fifteen. No, wait a minute. Fifteen and a half.'

'Ah, well. Mr Wilcox, aren't you ever amused at the solemnity with which we middle classes approach the subject of houses?'

They proceeded to the drawing-room. Chelsea managed better here. It was sallow and ineffective. One could visualize the ladies withdrawing to it, while their lords discussed life's realities below, to the accompaniment of cigars. Had Mrs Wilcox's drawing-room looked thus at Howards End? Just as this thought entered Margaret's brain, Mr Wilcox did ask her to be his wife, and the knowledge that she had been right so overcame her that she nearly fainted. (pp. 166–7)

At this stage in the novel, Margaret is growing increasingly desperate at the inability of her family to find a new home. She is attracted by Henry Wilcox's practical energy and, when invited to London to see his house in Ducie Street, she already suspects the real reason for his interest in her affairs. This is a lengthy passage because I want to show how Forster sets up complex eddies and cross-currents that play across the surface of his deceptively simple prose. Basically he is showing us here the contrast between Schlegel and Wilcox values; he does this mainly through gender distinctions, contrasting the cultivated female good taste of women like the Schlegel sisters against the philistine bad taste of the Wilcox business ethic. The interior of the house is used to demonstrate this tension and reveal Margaret's ambivalent attitude towards these robust but crude Wilcoxes and what they represent. Clearly the purpose of such a passage is to prepare Margaret (and the reader) for Henry's proposal and to make her acceptance of it plausible. The eventual marriage between the two of them is the most obvious form of 'connection' in the novel and, given their very different attitudes to life, the most difficult for us, the readers, to accept.

The details of the first paragraph are selected to show the tasteless opulence of the Wilcox décor, and contrast it with 'Chelsea' restraint. The 'sumptuous dado', 'the gilded wall-paper, amid whose foliage parrots sang', the heavy chairs and sideboard loaded ostentatiously with presentation plate are contrasted with the aesthetic discipline and muted, natural tones – the 'self-colour and self-denial' – that Margaret is used to. The dining-room and the entrance-hall also express the Wilcoxes' agressive maleness and their devotion to the Empire. This is done in a comical and deflationary way by the omniscient narrator. The furniture stands up to the competition of the appalling wall-paper 'like men', and the maroon leather chairs are like the offspring of a motor car. This last is a particularly telling criticism as well as being amusing because, as you may have noticed, Forster always associates the car with Wilcox selfishness and their abuse of power. Forster also notes the alliance between bourgeois acquisitiveness and imperial greed. The Duth Bible is Charles's trophy from the Boer War and 'Such a room admitted loot'. The entrance hall where 'We fellows smoke' is whole-heartedly masculine and the Gillray cartoons are an entirely appropriate detail. James Gillray was a coarse, crudely patriotic, political cartoonist during the Napoleonic Wars, so they too are suggestive of a public world of power and politics.

Margaret's equivocal attitude towards all this ugly splendour is delicately indicated. Her response at this vulnerable period in her life is to romanticise it. Indeed, rather like Helen at the beginning of the novel, she finds herself susceptible to Wilcox male strength and confidence in a manner that is unmistakably sexual. She persuades herself that there is a natural link between the modern business man and the warriors and hunters from the heroic past. There is something faintly absurd in her attempt to associate Henry with romantic thoughts of ancient liege lords, guest-halls and thanes out of the ancient sagas but, on the other hand, she isn't so seduced by his masterful comforts as to lose her critical judgement entirely. She only half-agrees with Henry when it would have been easier to go along with his coaxing insinuations about comfort. As so often in the novel, she attempts to mediate between extremes with scrupulous fairness. Material comfort and security do matter, but not to the exclusion of everything else. This is indicated by the teasing question that, in her turn, she puts to Henry concerning the anxious seriousness with which the middle classes approach matters of property, a question that, significantly, doesn't get an answer.

In the last paragraph, Forster once again uses interior decoration to suggest Wilcox attitudes, this time towards women. The drawing room is seen as exclusively a female preserve. It may be in better taste but it is feeble and 'ineffective'; 'sallow' suggests pallid ill-health. It is, literally, a 'with-drawing' room; here women retreat from life's challenges while their 'lords' get on with the real business of living downstairs. Wilcox men may be chivalrous and solicitous towards their women but they also marginalise them by protecting them from 'life's realities'.

So we can see that in the space of about a page, Forster maps out a whole set of contrasting attitudes; not only are the sophisticated but rather effete values of cultivated Chelsea compared to the full-blooded tastelessness of the commercial middle class, but the Wilcoxes' own view of themselves and the proper relationship between the sexes is also suggested.

The passage is skilfully economic in itself but it is also part of subtle on-going debate. If you replace this extract in the context of the chapter from which it comes, I think you will see this. A little earlier, Margaret tells Henry about Helen's fantasy about furniture: that it alone endures while men and houses perish, 'and that in the end the world will be a desert of chairs and sofas' (p. 165). This idea takes up a theme elaborated throughout the novel; namely, that modern life is so unsatisfactory because it is rootless and nomadic. We live in what Forster calls 'a civilization of luggage' (p. 154) and have lost touch with the earth. So the substantiality of the Wilcox furniture – those 'heavy chairs' and that 'immense' sideboard – mask a deep failure; because of their grasping materiality, the Wilcoxes cannot possess or own anything adequately. They are always camping and restlessly moving on through a series of temporary homes – Howards End, Ducie Street and now it is to be Oniton. They are very far removed from the ancient warriors of Margaret's imagination, dispensing largesse to their thanes. However, if substantial things prove insubstantial, the reverse is also true. The spirit of Mrs Wilcox and the house that Margaret has never seen are pervasive. The fact that Henry proposes just as Margaret is thinking of them both doesn't seem accidental. We are persuaded that there are mysteries in life that lie beneath the material surface of things, and their expression is more than coincidence. The manner of Henry's declaration underlines this. It is a shocking surprise that is also no surprise; impersonal and casual, it occurs in mid-sentence.

I'd like to conclude by looking at the role of the narrator in the passage. I find this very evasive and subtle. The narrator has a complex, shifting attitude towards Margaret herself, as well as the scene that she is surveying. There's no doubt that the Wilcox dining-room is hideous and it is generally viewed from the standpoint of an ironic aestheticism that seems to belong to 'Chelsea' bohemianism, yet this impression requires qualification when one looks closer. Good taste also has its fads and conformities; it sacrifices 'pluck' as well as comfort; it winces and refrains in a manner that seems feeble and over-fastidious. Beauty for beauty's sake it seems, is not an entire, unqualified good. Margaret views the energetic bad taste of the Wilcoxes 'with relief', but her sentimental attitude to the modern capitalist is not shared by the narrator. The flat critical judgement of 'Such a room admitted loot' seems to be his rather than hers. Again, there is the cool, ironic echo of Henry's bluff joviality – 'we fellows' – and there's little doubt that the narrator does not share Margaret's indulgent view of the leather arm chairs as 'jolly'.

These ambiguities of judgement and subtle shifts in tone mean that we come away from the passage with a sense of real differences between the pair but also of possible points of contact. Henry is anxious to please Margaret and she is not indifferent to him or his world. This does not mean that the narrator necessarily endorses a relationship between Margaret and Henry, or backs away from the problems it will entail.

Let us move on now to another passage, and a very different house.

5 Select a fourth passage for discussion

Desolation greeted her. Dirty finger-prints were on the hall-windows, flue and rubbish on its unwashed boards. The civilization of luggage had been here for a month, and then decamped. Dining-room and drawing-room – right and left – were guessed only by their wall-papers. They were just rooms where one could shelter from the rain. Across the ceiling of each ran a great beam. The dining-room and the hall revealed theirs openly, but the drawing-room's was match-boarded – because the facts of life must be concealed from ladies? Drawing-room, dining-room, and hall – how petty the names sounded! Here were simply three rooms where children could play and friends shelter from the rain. Yes, and they were beautiful.

Then she opened one of the doors opposite – there were two – and exchanged wall-papers for whitewash. It was the servants' part, though she scarcely realized that: just rooms again, where friends might shelter. The garden at the back was full of flowering cherries and plums. Farther on were hints of the meadow and a black cliff of pines. Yes, the meadow was beautiful.

Penned in by the desolate weather, she recaptured the sense of space which the motor had tried to rob from her. She remembered again that ten square miles are not ten times as wonderful as one square mile, that a thousand square miles are not practically the same as heaven. The phantom of bigness, which London encourages, was laid for ever when she paced from the hall at Howards End to its kitchen and heard the rains run this way and that where the watershed of the roof divided them. (p. 201)

Here we have Margaret's first view of Howards End. After her engagement, she and Henry travel down to Hertfordshire to see it; while he has gone for the key, she discovers that the door is open and goes in alone. I would say that the tensions in the passage revolve around absences and presences; the absence of human life, but also the absence of restless activity and human division, and the presence of calm intimacy, of self-sufficiency and self-acceptance. In its neglected state, Howards End seems full of potential and is a strangely magical space; a place for friends to shelter, where parents and children, masters and servants, society and nature can meet.

The initial impression is one of 'desolation' and exploitation: the 'civilization of luggage' has been and gone, leaving dirty finger marks, flue, rubbish and unwashed boards. The function of rooms can only be guessed by their wall-papers. But, paradoxically, even in its emptiness, the house has a mysterious, latent life; the friends, the ladies in the drawing-room and the playing children have a ghostly presence. The drawing-room and dining-room are 'just rooms' providing shelter from the elements, but their spartan state is in itself an admonishment of the costly and divisive decoration of the reception rooms at Ducie Street. The movement from wall-papers to whitewash acknowledges social degree but in a way that one 'scarcely realised'; the servants' quarters are 'just rooms again'. Margaret fantasised about warriors, guest-halls and thanes at Ducie Street, but the 'great beam' here seems to express, much more authentically, an ancient tradition of shelter and hospitality. The interior architecture expresses a fine disdain of 'petty' distinctions even though the Wilcoxes have left the imprint of their attitudes to class and gender by match-boarding the main constructional feature in the drawing-room in deference to their 'ladies'.

The last paragraph goes on to develop a distinction between restless diffusion or flux, and a rooted contentment. The second passage that we looked at showed us something of Forster's attitude to the modern city and here the empty house provides a quiet admonishment to the 'civilization of luggage'; the Wilcoxes have moved on taking their baggage with them. If we remember the exotic, tropical wall-paper and the Dutch Bible at Ducie Street, it is clear that, as empire builders and consumers, they are prepared to expand and range in many directions in search of their fulfilment.

But for Forster, it would seem that the best chance of happiness and contentment lies in the small scale of the familiar and domestic; within the few yards that Margaret paces between hall and kitchen at Howards End, she recaptures a true sense of space and a better awareness of time. She had lost both these on her journey down to Hilton in Henry's motor. Remember that the landscape had 'heaved and merged like porridge. Presently it congealed. They had arrived' (p. 199). Now the 'desolate weather' may pen her in physically, but the house seems magically to release her spiritually. The passage ends with her at the heart of some mystery, at one with herself under the centre of the roof where the rain waters part. Indeed, if the Wilcoxes' house in Ducie Street 'admitted loot' (p. 167) and was brashly male, there is something female about this house with its suggestion of hidden riches, subtle deferrals, sly vistas, and mysteriously opening doors.

I've suggested some implicit comparisons between Howards End and the Wilcox house at Ducie Street that we looked at in the last passage. You might care to add to these by looking at other passages where Forster deals with the Schlegel home at Wickham Place or the Wilcoxes' country house at Oniton. Descriptions of houses and attitudes to place seem very important in this novel. Broadly, I think we can say that the Schlegels appreciate their homes and the Wilcoxes exploit theirs. This is evident in the Oniton chapters that follow on from this one. Margaret is responsive to the scenery and the mysteries of the Welsh border; she would like to make it her home. Henry is merely out to make a splash; he soon wearies of the place, finds fault with it and moves on, just as he has left Howards End and Ducie Street before.

The Wilcox business ethic, their life of conspicuous consumption and exploitation of resources, seems to condemn them to a rootless, superficial way of life pursuing 'the phantom of bigness' (p. 201). The Schlegels, cosmopolitan and half-German, are born without strong native roots, live in a rented London house, but still seek to anchor themselves where they can. Margaret shows an appreciation of nature here, the fertile garden, the meadow and the pines that seem to form the appropriate and necessary context for the house; the Wilcoxes show no appreciation or feeling for nature whatever – save, of course, for Mrs Wilcox, whose house it was and whose ghost still lingers.

In one of those strange unexpected shocks and twists in the narrative in which this novel excels, Margaret is suddenly confronted by the mysterious Miss Avery at the end of this chapter. The old lady cares for the house in its neglected state and mistakes her for its former owner. The inference is clear: Margaret is the true owner of the house. As the spiritual successor to Mrs Wilcox, Howards End is her destiny and her resting place. All that is in the future, however, and there is still a third of the book to go. Margaret must go through disappointment and threatened scandal at Oniton, the challenge of Helen's pregnancy, disillusionment with Henry and the shock of Leonard Bast's death, before she can take up her rightful inheritance. At the moment the house is empty; on her next visit, the Schlegel furniture will be mysteriously and appropriately in place. Only after much grief and pain, will house, furniture and people finally come together to make a new life and a fresh beginning.

We have looked at four passages that feature Margaret and I think it is now time to stand back and take a broader view of what we've achieved and what we still need to do.

6   *Have I achieved a sufficiently complex sense of the novel?*

I think it would be a rather lazy or incurious reader who could give a simple affirmative to this question on the strength of studying four passages, but we have made some progress. For a start, we have a better grasp on Margaret's role as mediator between two opposing philosophies of life and a gathering awareness of what these two philosophies stand for. Crudely, the Wilcoxes get things done but are tasteless and destructive, the Schlegels value culture, the private life and revere the past, but are ineffectual in the public world and so powerless to influence events. Howards End itself functions as some kind of symbol of England's collective past that is in jeopardy. It needs to be saved and protected from the worst excesses of the modern world and in return it will exert its spiritual power as a reconciling and healing agent. What at one level appears a small scale domestic drama between two middle-class families involving the inheritance of a house, is, at another, nothing less than a struggle for the soul of England itself. Howards End *is* England – or, at least a particular version of England that Forster feels passionately is at risk and must be preserved.

A study of Margaret's role will certainly get us into the centre of this struggle for England's soul but the novel is spatially expansive, and we need to see Margaret's involvement with Henry in the context of a wide range of relationships in order to do justice to Forster's ambitions as a social novelist. It isn't just a simple tale of courtship and marriage, though this does provide the narrative thread for most of the book. Margaret's relationship with her sister Helen, for example, is intense and ultimately proves stronger than her feelings for her husband. Other members of the two families – Charles Wilcox, Evie, and Dolly on one side, Tibby Schlegel, Aunt Juley and the German cousins on the other – all have their part to play in Forster's sense of 'the Condition of England' just before the First World War. But, of course, the one really significant omission from this list is the down-trodden city clerk, Leonard Bast; no analysis of *Howards End* would begin to be adequate without a careful consideration of Leonard's role in the novel, why Forster felt compelled to include him, and whether he has adequately solved the problems and complications that Leonard brings to his analysis of English life at this critical time in English history.

Leonard is important structurally and thematically; he is a third social element that complicates the neat symmetrical relationship between the other two. He introduces the lower classes into the novel and all the problems that they must bring to the liberal establishment; his relationship with Helen is also an important counterweight to the marriage between Margaret and Henry. Moreover, if his existence complicates the novel, it also provides its crisis and resolution. There are other aspects of *Howards End* that interest me; for example, the way the novel manages to be both 'a good story' that involves us in a sense of felt life, but is also shown to be a fictional game apart from life. The symbolic patterning in the novel seems to pull against the psychological plausibility of its characters at critical moments and it is not at all clear to me whether this is an unintentional weakness, or an essential part of the novel's strategy. Also the tidiness of the plot seems to be resisted, even defeated, by the openness and tentativeness of the language. These are complex issues but I think we can make some progress with them, particularly if we focus on the problem of Leonard Bast.

II Aspects of the novel

After the initial drama of Helen's failed romance with Paul Wilcox, a new phase in the novel begins in Chapter 5 when the Schlegels visit the Queen's Hall for a concert. Forster, with deft social and psychological insight, shows us the various attitudes and prejudices of each of the listeners to the main event of the evening, a playing of Beethoven's Fifth Symphony, but it is Helen's response to the music that is dwelt on most extensively and is the most revealing. Here is a passage from that chapter.

Helen said to her aunt: 'Now comes the wonderful movement: first of all the goblins, and then a trio of elephants dancing'; and Tibby implored the company generally to look out for the transitional passage on the drums.
'On the what, dear?'
'On the *drum*, Aunt Juley.'
'No; look out for the part where you think you have done with the goblins and they come back,' breathed Helen, as the music started with a goblin walking quietly over the universe, from end to end. Others followed him. They were not aggressive creatures; it was that that made them so terrible to Helen. They merely observed in passing that there was no such thing as splendour or heroism in the world. After the interlude of elephants dancing, they returned and made the observation for the second time. Helen could not contradict them, for, once at all events, she had felt the same, and had seen the reliable walls of youth collapse. Panic and emptiness! Panic and emptiness! The goblins were right.
Her brother raised his finger: it was the transitional passage on the drum.
For, as if things were going too far, Beethoven took hold of the goblins and made them do what he wanted. He appeared

in person. He gave them a little push, and they began to walk in major key instead of in a minor, and then – he blew with his mouth and they were scattered! Gusts of splendour, gods and demi-gods contending with vast swords, colour and fragrance broadcast on the field of battle, magnificent victory, magnificent death! Oh, it all burst before the girl, and she even stretched out her gloved hands as if it were tangible. Any fate was titanic; any contest desirable; conqueror and conquered would alike be applauded by the angels of the utmost stars.

And the goblins – they had not really been there at all? They were only the phantoms of cowardice and unbelief? One healthy human impulse would dispel them? Men like the Wilcoxes, or President Roosevelt, would say yes. Beethoven knew better. The goblins really had been there. They might return – and they did. It was as if the splendour of life might boil over and waste to steam and froth. In its dissolution one heard the terrible, ominous note, and a goblin, with increased malignity, walked quietly over the universe from end to end. Panic and emptiness! Panic and emptiness! Even the flaming ramparts of the world might fall. (pp. 46–7)

This is a strange passage to come across when you first read the novel, and doesn't seem to have much relevance to anything else that is going on; rather excessive and overblown in its language, it appears to be something of a digression on Beethoven that Forster has inserted for his own pleasure. It's only when you begin to study the book more closely that its significance becomes apparent. It works on several levels.

First, part of the purpose of the chapter from which this is taken is to show us how people who have supposedly come together for a shared, common experience, use the cultural stimulus of 'Beethoven' for different ends: even culture, Forster shows, is not the healer and 'connector' that it is made out to be. It feeds the patriotism of the German cousins and it gives Aunt Juley vague moral uplift while making her uncomfortable; Margaret, level-headed as ever, appreciates the music as music but Tibby's interest is fastidiously technical and Helen's response, as we see here, is wildly imaginative. The first part of the passage shows the satirical side of Forster as poor Aunt Juley struggles to get to grips with the music. We find her uncomprehending struggles and Tibby's precious attitude amusing but, as we move further into the passage, Helen's response gives us more difficulty, partly because it seems to become the narrator's also. There's an uncertainty of tone here which makes for an uncertainty of response; this may be accidental or it may be by design; it is certainly unsettling. What starts as fanciful whimsy becomes, by the end, ominous prophesy of a quite different order of seriousness as we move away from the comfortable, cosy, social world of the known to a mysterious, unseen world that is larger than life, a world of 'gods and demi-gods', 'vast swords', a 'field of battle', 'titanic' conquests and 'flaming ramparts'.

Helen experiences the music as a vision of life. She translates the music into pictures and a narrative that expresses a heroic conflict between chaos and order, negative meaninglessness and triumphant conquest. The modulations in the imagery are sudden and surprising. The rather dotty idea of 'the trio of elephants dancing' with which the passage begins gives way to the eerie notion of a goblin 'walking quietly over the universe, from end to end', merely observing 'in passing' that there is 'no such thing as splendour or heroism in the world'. Art may express a yearning for 'magnificent victory, magnificent death' but the goblins will always return to waste the splendour of life. Beneath all human achievement lie 'Panic and emptiness', whatever the confident people in power – the Wilcoxes and Roosevelts – may say.

The second level of analysis, then, is what this passage tells us about Helen. It tells us that her disappointment with Paul is still alive in her; she has seen 'the reliable walls of youth collapse' and knows the goblins are right. But she resists this knowledge with all her considerable energy for life and natural idealism. Her vision of life as a heroic battle with noble possibilities for victor and vanquished alike, is very much the key to her behaviour and role in the novel overall. She is the one who makes brief but powerful 'connections' with both the wealthy Wilcoxes and the penniless Basts; she is the more purely quixotic of the two sisters when it comes to the matter of money and men. She struggles with her more practical sister against Henry Wilcox's crude materialism for most of the novel, and, in a sense, it is a battle that she wins, for the sibling relationship proves the stronger in the end.

Crudely, Helen is the engine of the plot; she makes everything 'happen' except Margaret's decision to marry Henry. Margaret reflects but Helen acts. It is her carelessness with Leonard's umbrella that brings him into the Schlegel's world during this chapter; it is her outrage and impetuosity that reveals Henry's infidelity at Oniton and her pregnancy that shows his double standards later at Howards End. She forces Margaret to stay in the house with her against orthodox marital obligation, so causing Leonard's death and Charles's imprisonment. This, of course, will lead to Henry's collapse and the final victory of the 'inner life'. Small wonder that she stretches out her gloved hand here as if to touch the glory of Beethoven's musical victory or that her imagination is so vivid. She is the most destructive but also the most creative agency in the novel. Part of the message in the music seems to be that you cannot have the one in life without the other. This brings us to the third level of analysis; what the passage can tell us about Forster himself, and his view of the purpose of art.

The sentiments expressed in the passage are nominally Helen's, it is her head that we are supposed to be inside, but there seems to be a move away to a more universal statement of the nature of human life towards the end. In other words, if the goblins are real for Helen, they are real for Forster also. Moreover, by talking about the effect of Beethoven's music on Helen, the narrator is also talking, more generally, about the challenges and difficulties of writing too. Forster, like Beethoven or any creative artist, has the problems of reconciling truth with art. I would suggest that *Howards End* is not a confident text; there's a sense of doubt and fear, insecurity and danger, throughout: 'the goblin footfall' (p. 57) that the narrator refers to at the end of this chapter reverberates throughout the book. This ominous warning is partly social. Beneath the elegant surface of this novel which deals with the comfortable lives of the well-off, there lies a very different reality; this is the world of the deprived urban poor, the abject life in the great city slums that were a feature of Edwardian society – what Forster, in the language of the times, calls 'the abyss'. Leonard's life is the nearest we get to this reality, and significantly, it is in this chapter that he is introduced. But 'the goblin footfall' is also metaphysical; Forster reveals a sense of despair in this passage that goes beyond social guilt to a vision of the ultimate meaninglessness of all human endeavour and struggle – 'the splendour of life might boil over and waste to steam and froth.' This indeed is a vision of 'panic and emptiness' for the writer; it renders language itself powerless and impotent in its attempt to give shape and meaning to the world. How is one to write when victories and defeats alike are meaningless?

Forster acknowledges but resists such nihilistic thoughts. This passage goes some way to explain the strange paradox that while Forster's style in this novel is always open, provisional, even insecure, he also manipulates and shapes its events with an obvious arbitrariness. He never bothers to conceal the fact that *Howards End* is a piece of constructed fiction. Like Beethoven, he will take hold of the goblins of doubt and despair in this novel because he feels, similarly, that it is the duty of art to scatter them with 'gusts of splendour', to show that there are great causes in life to fight and die for. But the goblins will always return; it is the duty of the artist to acknowledge this too. So, to summarise, Forster is really putting down a prospectus in this passage for the novel as a whole. Beethoven's struggle is also his struggle; he is showing that, as a writer, he too must be open to the fact that life is messy, inconclusive, and probably meaningless, but still give a voice to human aspiration, expose social evil, and provide the consolation of meaningful artistic form.

I'd like to move on now and take a look at Leonard Bast after Forster had followed him back home after the concert to his sordid flat in Camelia Road.

Leonard was trying to form his style on Ruskin: he understood him to be the greatest master of English Prose. He read forward steadily, occasionally making a few notes.

'Let us consider a little each of these characters in succession, and first (for of the shafts enough has been said already), what is very peculiar to this church – its luminousness.'

Was there anything to be learnt from this fine sentence? Could he introduce it, with modifications, when he next wrote a letter to his brother, the lay-reader? For example –

'Let us consider a little each of these characters in succession, and first (for of the absence of ventilation enough has been said already), what is very peculiar to this flat – its obscurity.'

Something told him that the modification would not do; and that something, had he known it, was the spirit of English

Prose. 'My flat is dark as well as stuffy.' Those were the words for him.

And the voice in the gondola rolled on, piping melodiously of Effort and Self-Sacrifice, full of high purpose, full of beauty, full even of sympathy and the love of men, yet somehow eluding all that was actual and insistent in Leonard's life. For it was the voice of one who had never been dirty or hungry, and had not guessed successfully what dirt and hunger are. (pp. 61–2)

This is a particularly interesting passage, because it illustrates several failures of 'connection'. Leonard is looking for something to give significance and meaning to his dreary, unfulfilling life. He goes to concerts, visits art-galleries and reads great writers. He has just returned from the performance of Beethoven's Fifth Symphony that had moved Helen so profoundly that she had gone home early, inadvertently taking his umbrella with her. Leonard is poor, an umbrella is a symbol of his gentility and one which he can ill-afford to lose; consequently he spends the rest of the concert worrying about his loss. The connection between money and culture is clear; the exclusiveness of the one without the comfort and support of the other is something that Forster continues to explore in this passage.

Leonard is self-consciously studying a literary text. Not because it speaks to him directly, but because he has picked up somewhere the idea that Ruskin is 'the greatest master of English Prose'. The 'fine sentence' that he reads is courteous in tone and elaborately constructed. It is the work of a writer with time and leisure, and intended for a reader who also enjoys a comfortable existence. The comradely 'us' that forms the subject of the sentence implies two connoisseurs of Venetian architecture – or one connoisseur instructing his pupil. The details of church architecture in Italy can hardly be of much interest to Leonard; someone who worries about the loss of an umbrella is never going to afford foreign travel.

The inappropriateness of the whole exercise is underlined by the comic parody that follows. This serves to illustrate that such a style of writing has no possible use in Leonard's daily existence nor could be made serviceable to his needs. Forster keeps the syntactic frame of the original sentence and inserts another vocabulary more akin to Leonard's present environment but still elaborately and loftily removed from daily life. This modification is, of course, supposed to be Leonard's but this is sleight of hand for it is the narrator's exercise, on Leonard's behalf, to make the ironic point. Words like 'ventilation' and 'obscurity' elude all that is 'actual and insistent' in Leonard's life. This can only be honestly expressed in statements as flat and drab as can be: 'My flat is dark as well as stuffy.' In the last paragraph, the narrator goes on to mock the lofty moralisings of Ruskin, 'piping melodiously of Effort and Self-Sacrifice' from his gondola.

But the satire is interestingly double-edged. If Forster is criticising the failure of Ruskin, however well-intentioned his efforts, to reach the dirty and hungry, the passage also serves to highlight his own problems. Will he be any better at guessing what dirt and hunger are? Is he any less patronising? Forster's project in *Howards End* is to write a 'Condition of England' novel, that is a fiction that seriously engages with the social problems of the time. Undoubtedly the living conditions of the poor in London and the other major cities in Britain were a major social issue during the Edwardian period; without some attempt to engage with this problem, Forster's efforts would lose all credibility. He is honest enough at the beginning of this chapter to admit that for him the 'very poor' are 'unthinkable' (p. 58), so Leonard's aspirations to culture and gentility are his attempt to broaden the range and add some depth to his social analysis. But even going this far out of the affluent world of the Schlegels and Wilcoxes gives Forster some awkward difficulties because it exposes the limitations of his liberal philosophy of life and the kind of writing that this underpins.

I think the ambiguity of a phrase like 'the spirit of English Prose' illustrates Forster's difficulties quite well. One might ask oneself the question, 'whose England – and whose prose?' Like the Schlegels, Forster had a private income guaranteed by the thriving capitalists of the period. His standard of living and his culture were supported by the entrepreneurial energies of the Wilcoxes and their kind – whose values he deplored – and the sweated labours of the urban poor, like Leonard Bast. He has Margaret voice the anxieties and the bad conscience that such a situation must produce throughout the novel. Bluntly, a liberal philosophy of life wishes to defend an unjust economic system because it maintains a quality of life and a cultural tradition that is felt to be valuable and important to preserve; it wants to placate its social guilt over this by seeking ways to improve the lot of the many while still maintaining the privileges of the few. The fact of the matter is that this kind of well-meant social and literary philanthropy by the affluent is not going to make Leonard Bast's depressing life any better – and Forster well knew this, as he shows here.

Forster was writing in a tradition of middle-class liberalism that includes Ruskin and most of the great English writers of the nineteenth century. One might query if any of them captured the life and aspirations of the poor adequately. Forster is no different. Though he shows a sympathetic awareness of some of Leonard's difficulties, I don't think he quite 'connects' with him in a way that convinces. In social terms, Leonard remains stubbornly a case-history, rather remote from the elegances of Forster's fastidious prose. The nub of the problem is the language of literature itself. Forster implies that 'the spirit of English Prose' is truth and honesty which, when applied to Leonard Bast, means 'My flat is dark as well as stuffy'. There is a paradox here, however, and we need to understand its implications: these may be 'the words for him' but they are not the words for Forster's middle-class readers; a novel composed entirely of such language would be considered rather dull and wouldn't sell many copies.

It takes more than truth and honesty to make successful art. Good novels may have to have moments of plain, unvarnished truth and this one is no exception. One thinks of Leonard's 'unforgettable' negative when asked if the breaking of the dawn after his evening walk was wonderful (p. 126), or Margaret's blistering exposure of Henry's double moral standard (p. 300). But if a fiction is to achieve the status of literature and so become valuable and significant for Forster and his readers alike, it has also to be artful; *Howards End* is a sophisticated and crafted narrative containing many discourses – lyrical, satirical, polemical and patriotic, to name but a few. All of these could qualify as expressions of 'the spirit of English Prose', but most of them ignore Leonard Bast or are irrelevant to his problems. Forster makes it plain that the only language he feels can adequately express the plight of the genteel poor is the kind of drab documentary realism shown here: 'my flat is dark as well as stuffy.'

As much as Ruskin's prose, then, Forster's novel pipes 'melodiously', is full of love, purpose and sympathy, but, while noting the problem, is not much better at engaging with the 'actual and insistent' in Leonard's life, or doing anything about his hopeless situation. Indeed Leonard's very existence – and the language needed to express it adequately – threaten to undermine and destroy the book altogether. This passage shows us that Schlegel culture is going to fail Leonard – it is not going to help give meaning and significance to his existence – but, as the novel is written from a Schlegel-like point of view and with Schlegel-like assumptions, this will inevitably lead to a contradiction between the social conscience and the literary values of Forster himself.

How Forster handles this contradiction textually is best illustrated by looking at another passage. I'm going to move on now to the other end of the novel and the moment of Leonard's death in Chapter 41.

> He entered a garden, steadied himself against a motor-car that he found in it, found a door open and entered the house. Yes, it would be very easy. From a room to the left he heard voices, Margaret's amongst them. His own name was called aloud, and a man whom he had never seen said, 'Oh, is he there? I am not surprised. I now thrash him within an inch of his life.'
>
> 'Mrs Wilcox,' said Leonard, 'I have done wrong.'
>
> The man took him by the collar and cried, 'Bring me a stick.' Women were screaming. A stick, very bright, descended. It hurt him, not where it descended, but in the heart. Books fell over him in a shower. Nothing had sense.
>
> 'Get some water,' commanded Charles, who had all through kept very calm. 'He's shamming. Of course I only used the blade. Here, carry him out into the air.'
>
> Thinking that he understood these things, Margaret obeyed him. They laid Leonard, who was dead, on the gravel; Helen poured water over him.
>
> 'That's enough,' said Charles.
>
> 'Yes, murder's enough,' said Miss Avery, coming out of the house with the sword. (pp. 315–16)

This is the climax of the novel and a justly famous scene: it illustrates several characteristics that are typical of Forster's fictional world and shows how he uses his skills as a writer to resolve uncomfortable problems. There's a fine balance in the passage between chaos and order, lack of meaning and significance, that is intimately related to Forster's difficulties with Leonard.

We experience the first part from Leonard's point of view and 'Nothing had sense'. This is the resolution of his second night walk in the book as he wanders, confused and unknowing, into the supreme adventure that he has been yearning for. This proves to be an experience of sacrifice and expiation that is necessary for the book to find its own way to a satisfying conclusion. All that he experiences is vague and unspecified, which is appropriate for his poor state of health. He enters 'a garden' and rests himself against 'a motor-car', the symbol of Wilcox aggression that is to come. Charles, 'a man he had never seen', emerges from a muddled impression of places and voices to threaten him with a cliché of impersonal class disapproval that proves, in the event, to be an ironic understatement. The actual beating itself is taken out of the realm of squalid reality into something more ritual and mysterious. Though he is grabbed by the collar and women scream, the stick is 'very bright' and hurts him 'in the heart'. He dies confused and denied all meaning in a 'shower' of books.

The second part of the passage shifts the perspective to a neutral overview of the scene but the mysterious quality remains. Charles's confident commands are contradicted by the narrator's casual statement of Leonard's death, and Helen's action has the ritual effect of a libation which ironically echoes the 'shower' of books earlier. The climax of the scene is the sudden appearance of Miss Avery, carrying the Schlegel sword like the archangel Michael who banished Adam and Eve from the garden of Eden. She is the spiritual guardian of Howards End seeking retribution and, in her hands, the sword shifts from being an instrument of violence to a symbol of justice.

So this is the moment when three families and three social groups come together at Howards End to complete a tragic pattern. Leonard has been failed by both Wilcoxes and Schlegels, and this seems to be symbolised by the manner in which Wilcox aggression and Schlegel culture combine to produce his death. In this way, Forster can both be truthful to his own insight into Leonard's hopeless predicament but also remove him from the scene. Bluntly, Leonard's death allows

Forster to give the text a pleasing aesthetic pattern and this is
indicated by the self-conscious manner in which Forster orches-
trates some of the novel's dominant symbols - the car, the books,
the sword, the character of Miss Avery - in the passage.
Moreover, as he does in the Beethoven passage we discussed
earlier, Forster moves suddenly from an ordinary domestic
context into a heroic one; Leonard is taken way from his petty
genteel world of lost umbrellas and caught up in a world of 'gods
and demi-gods', 'swords', 'conquests' and epic 'fields of battle'.

Leonard functions as both pathetic scapegoat and heroic
saviour. By giving him a tragic end, Forster not only removes his
troublesome unmet needs that are awkward, insoluble and ugly,
but also facilitates a swift and pleasing ending to his novel, for
Leonard's manslaughter removes the Wilcoxes as a threat to the
peace and stability of Howards End and allows Margaret to
finally take up her promised spiritual inheritance there.
Leonard dead is an infinitely more potent and imaginative force
than Leonard living. Forster is able to sentimentalise his 'yeo-
man' spirit as part of 'England's hope' (p. 314); he is also able to
salve his conscience by making Leonard's son the inheritor of
Howard's End, and so the promise for a better, more socially
united future for a country torn by industrialism and class
division.

Much has been written about the relative success or failure of
the novel's final pages and you will have to make up your own
mind. I should just like to conclude this section by pointing out
that the fine balance between order and chaos, hope and
despair, that I have been suggesting is an important aspect of
the text, continues to the end. Forster chooses to close his novel
with reassuring images of marriage, family continuity and
home. But any scrutiny will reveal just how tenuous, how
arbitrary, these 'connections' are. By the end, Henry is a broken
man, and the family at Howards End is a strangely unorthodox
one. Its domestic harmony and peace can only be achieved by
subduing the energies of the main characters and by withdrawing them from history and all the forces that are shaping the
modern world into an enclave of vulnerable pastoralism; the
promise of harvest which is the novel's final triumphant symbol
is simultaneously qualified by the threat of advancing urbanism
with its attendant images of destruction and decay. I think you
will find that the tidiness of Forster's solution continues to be

resisted, even defeated, by the tentativeness of the language with which he expresses it.

Many readers have found this open-handedness irritating, particularly when it is combined with a 'happy' ending that seems strained – almost brutal – and only achieved by an abrupt withdrawal from the world, and those forces making for social change that Forster has so accurately depicted during the course of the novel. A more positive reading might be to see the end of the novel as an expression of hope, or yearning aspiration, for a different sort of society and a different kind of future. The symbolic patterning that is so insistent in the book may indeed work against the psychological plausibility of the characterisation, but an important aspect of Forster's endeavours as a novelist is to show that hope and desire cannot always be expressed through an accurate description of the world as we recognise it; some bold, imaginative transformation is required – despite the artistic risks that this entails. This is necessary in order that Forster can suggest other worlds and other possibilities to the one we feel compelled to live and choose in.

7
The Indian Novel:
A Passage to India (1924)

I Constructing an overall analysis

A gap of fourteen years and a World War separates *A Passage to India* from Forster's other novels. It is his last novel, and generally regarded as his finest; indeed, many consider it to be a classic of twentieth-century fiction. A short summary of the plot will show us certain features that are familiar to those who have read some of Forster's earlier novels, as well as some interesting new developments.

1 *After reading the novel, think about the story and what kind of pattern you can see in the text*

The setting is India at the time of the Raj. Mrs Moore and her prospective daughter-in-law, Adela Quested, are newly arrived in Chandrapore, an insignificant town in Imperial India, where Mrs Moore's son, Ronny Heaslop, has the post of City Magistrate. The purpose of the visit is to make the engagement official, if Adela is sure of her feelings. Adela is an independent, serious-minded girl who wants to see the 'real India'. The English community oblige her by arranging a formal 'Bridge Party' where she can meet some of the local Indians. This is not a success, but Mrs Moore has already struck up a warm friendship with a young Moslem doctor, Aziz, who she has met, by chance, in a mosque. Matters develop further when Cyril Fielding, the liberal Principal of the local Government College, invites the two ladies to meet Aziz and Professor Godbole, one of his Brahman colleagues, at a tea party. Unfortunately this, too, is a failure when

Ronny's arrival sours the atmosphere and the party breaks up in some disorder. Adela has decided that India has changed Ronny and she no longer wishes to marry him, but a mysterious car accident brings them closer together and they announce their engagement. Meanwhile, Aziz and Fielding have taken to each other and, by the end of the first section of the novel, have become close friends.

The second part of the novel revolves around the mysterious Marabar Caves some twenty miles out of Chandrapore. Aziz has impulsively invited the English ladies to visit these local curiosities at Fielding's tea party and feels compelled to go through with his scheme although no one is very enthusiastic. From the start, the expedition is dogged with misfortune: Fielding and Godbole are late and miss the train; Mrs Moore is upset by the caves and becomes unwell; Aziz and Adela continue to a high rock called the Kawa Dol with a single guide, but become separated and enter different caves. Aziz emerges from his to find that Adela has gone down the hill and returned to Chandrapore in a passing car. Fielding arrives late and the party returns home to discover that Aziz has been charged with attempted rape. Attitudes in the community polarise and harden. Fielding, confident of Aziz's innocence, resigns from the English Club and throws in his lot with the Indians. Mrs Moore is similarly certain that Aziz is not guilty but, ill and disillusioned, she decides to go home to England early and dies at sea. Finally, the matter is brought to trial where, by being forced to re-live the experience, Adela becomes convinced that she has made a mistake and withdraws the charge. Much recrimination follows and Adela is shunned by the Anglo-Indian community. Fielding feels bound to support her and, in consequence, his friendship with Aziz suffers. This part of the novel ends with Adela and Fielding returning separately to England.

The narrative concludes, two years later, in the native state of Mau where Aziz has taken up a post as doctor to the Rajah. Professor Godbole is also there as Minister of Education. It is the monsoon season and Godbole is busy officiating in Gokul Ashtami, a major Hindu festival celebrating the birth of Krishna. Fielding, back in India and promoted, has arrived in an official capacity to inspect the new school. Aziz has no wish to meet him as he feels betrayed. Because of misunderstandings and resentments, he is convinced that Fielding has married Adela after persuading him to forgo the financial compensation from her that was his due. He discovers that this is untrue: Fielding has married Stella, Mrs Moore's daughter by her second husband, but Aziz is not mollified until he falls under the spell of Ralph, Mrs Moore's other son. Although diffident and eccentric, Ralph reminds Aziz of Mrs Moore and the special relationship that they enjoyed. Reconciliation follows when the boats carrying Aziz and Fielding over the great Mau Tank collide at the height of the festivities pitching them both into the water. The novel ends with the pair enjoying one last ride together through the Mau jungle, knowing that their friendship cannot be sustained in the complexities of modern India.

If we stand back and look at the book as a whole, we can see that the pattern of this plot is reminiscent of Forster's earlier Italian novels; two rather insular English women, a young *ingénue* accompanied by her older chaperone, visit a foreign country where they rapidly get out of their depth. They react badly to strange occurrences that test their somewhat limited moral and spiritual capacities. After some sort of breakdown, they return home. One dies *en route*, the other, chastened and wiser, has to try and build a new life. Taking the hint from Adela's surname of 'Quested', it would seem that the plot of this story is a 'quest'; a journey that exposes the weakness and vulnerability of English middle-class virtue when it becomes isolated in an alien, unsympathetic land.

Other clues to the theme might be found in the title of the novel, for 'passage' is a loaded word. At the most obvious level it refers to a sea-voyage, the mode of travel that was necessary to get to India at the time that this novel is set. But the title also includes the idea of 'rites of passage' where a 'passage' is an initiation ceremony, often taxing and painful, into a more complex mode of existence. Finally, the title contains a reference to the nineteenth-century poet, Walt Whitman, who wrote a poem called 'Passage to India'. Forster admired Whitman greatly but I think there is some measure of irony in his decision to echo the poet in his own title.

Whitman's poem is a buoyant, optimistic exhortation to create global communication and marry the Western to the Eastern world through the opening of the Suez canal; it is typical of its time in its praise of, and confidence in, the power of modern technology to remove obstacles and solve problems. It sees such triumphs as heralding even greater victories of the spirit when mankind will make a passage to 'more than India' and create universal brotherhood. Forster's sadder, twentieth-century novel, seems to cast a shadow on such hopes, to show the impossibility of connection between people of different cultures and creeds in a hopelessly divided world. In this respect Forster's last novel is more pessimistic than his earlier fiction.

This idea of people reaching out for meaningful connection but being frustrated and disappointed, is much in evidence throughout the story, and seems to be an essential part of its pattern. Adela is considering marriage and wants to see 'the real India', but her attempts to complete both projects end in disaster; the failure of the 'Bridge Party' and Fielding's tea party lead to catastrophe in the ominous Marabar Caves, which in turn leads to her eventual social ostracism and the break-up of her engagement. Her failure to find love with Ronny is duplicated by Aziz and Fielding in their unsuccessful attempt to cross the racial divide and make a lasting friendship. Both these relationships are seen in a social context that is hopelessly divisive, for colonial India is full of mistrust and racial hatred. Only the friendship between Aziz and Mrs Moore gives any grounds for optimism, and this seems an odd, rather unlikely bond between two people divided by age and race; based on one brief encounter early in the novel, it remains idealised, untested and incapable of any practical development.

Other thoughts that occur to me during this first, preliminary examination of the story include the strange organisation of the text. The novel is divided into three sections – 'Mosque', 'Caves' and 'Temple' – but the point and status of the last section is obscure, for the main drive of the narrative is directed towards, and through, the mysterious experiences in the Marabar Caves, the dramatic climax of Aziz's trial, and the vindication of his good name. The aftermath in Mau seems rather an anti-climax that diminishes the impact of an otherwise excellent conventional plot. The significance of the names of these sections and the reasons why Forster includes the curious Hindu festival at Mau, is something I must return to. First, I must get some more direct access into the novel.

2 *Select a short passage featuring one of the main characters and try to build upon the ideas you have established so far*

Now this gives me an interesting problem straight away. In most novels the main character is self-selecting but *A Passage to India* is curiously diffuse in this respect. Three characters – Adela, Fielding and Aziz – come immediately to mind, and I could base my basic analysis of the novel on any one of them but also be aware of its partial, limited nature. Fielding is honourable, decent and fair-minded, a fitting representative of those liberal humanistic values that Forster admired, but, though we learn much about his inner thoughts and feelings, his role in the book is curiously marginal and ineffectual. Aziz's character is the most detailed in presentation, and dominates the first and last sections, but Forster strangely withdraws him from the scene during the build-up to, and drama of, his trial – a crucial stage in the novel. Adela is central to the plot but leaves for England at the end of the 'Caves' section and plays no further part in the action. The friendship of Fielding and Aziz, and the abortive courtship of Adela and Ronny, are both essential to the pattern of the novel and both must be explored but I'm going to content myself here with an examination of the latter because, however attenuated, this seems to be the essential plot: Adela's search for 'the real India', her experience in the cave, her accusation and recantation, are the material substance of the novel on which everything else depends. I shall begin by looking at a passage from Chapter 5 (page references to the novel relate to the Penguin edition, 1989).

'Do kindly tell us who these ladies are,' asked Mrs Moore.

'You're superior to them, anyway. Don't forget that. You're superior to everyone in India except one or two of the Ranis, and they're on an equality.'

Advancing, she shook hands with the group and said a few words of welcome in Urdu. She had learnt the lingo, but only to speak to her servants, so she knew none of the politer forms and of the verbs only the imperative mood. As soon as her speech was over, she inquired of her companions, 'Is that what you wanted?'

'Please tell these ladies that I wish we could speak their language, but we have only just come to their country.'

'Perhaps we could speak yours a little,' one of the ladies said.

'Why, fancy, she understands!' said Mrs Turton.

'Eastbourne, Piccadilly, Hyde Park Corner,' said another of the ladies.

'Oh, yes, they're English-speaking.'

'But now we can talk: how delightful!' cried Adela, her face lighting up.

'She knows Paris also,' called one of the onlookers.

'They pass Paris on the way, no doubt,' said Mrs Turton, as if she was describing the movements of migratory birds. Her manner had grown more distant since she had discovered that some of the group were Westernized, and might apply her own standards to her.

'The shorter lady, she is my wife, she is Mrs Bhattacharya,' the onlooker explained. 'The taller lady, she is my sister, she is Mrs Das.'

The shorter and the taller ladies both adjusted their saris, and smiled. There was a curious uncertainty about their gestures, as if they sought for a new formula which neither East nor West could provide. When Mrs Bhattacharya's husband spoke, she turned away from him, but she did not mind seeing the other men. Indeed all the ladies were uncertain, cowering, recovering, giggling, making tiny gestures of atonement or despair at all that was said, and alternately fondling the terrier or shrinking from him. Miss Quested now had her desired opportunity; friendly Indians were before her, and she tried to make them talk, but she failed, she strove in vain against the echoing walls of their civility. Whatever she said produced a murmur of deprecation, varying into a murmur of concern when she dropped her pocket-handkerchief. She tried doing nothing, to see what that produced, and they too did nothing. Mrs Moore was equally unsuccessful. Mrs Turton waited for them with a detached expression; she had known what nonsense it all was from the first. (pp. 61–3)

At this point, in response to Adela's wish to see 'the real India', the Collector has organised a 'Bridge Party' – jokingly so called because it attempts to 'bridge' the gap between East and West – on the lawns of the English Club. It is in this formal context that Adela and Mrs Moore are introduced to some Indian ladies by the hostile and cynical Mrs Turton. There is obviously a tension

– a failure of communication – between the colonial power and
the subject races here that produces both comedy and pathos.
Mrs Turton has no intention of communicating with her per-
ceived inferiors while the two English visitors find their own
attempts frustrated by the constraints of the occasion.

I've chosen a lengthy passage because I wanted to illustrate
something of the range and flexibility of Forster's social criticism, and the way it can suddenly modulate into something
stranger, more mysterious. It begins with the broad comedy of
Mrs Turton's stupid and arrogant behaviour. She's shown to be
obsessed with her own status and crudely inept at Urdu. There's
delightful satire in the revelation that the Indian ladies are
better educated, more sophisticated and wider travelled than
she is, and in her discomfiture in this knowledge. What we have
at the beginning of the passage is a sharp comedy of manners
moving over the surface of things, catching the tone of the
verbal interchanges with all their incongruities, and interspers-
ing them with a deflating authorial commentary. Mrs Turton's
suburban lack of breeding and patronising sense of racial
superiority are well captured by mixing her sort of vocabulary
and phrasing like 'She had learnt the lingo' or 'Why, fancy, she
understands!' with the narrator's own ironic asides like 'she
knew none of the politer forms and of the verbs only the
imperative mood', or 'as if she was describing the movements of
migratory birds'. The broad humour of her complacent refusal
to communicate at all is also contrasted with the good natured
attempts of the cosmopolitan Indian ladies to find cultural
connections in their disparate list of place names – 'Eastbourne,
Piccadilly, Hyde Park Corner . . . Paris' – which is comical in a
rather different way for it shows the inherent difficulties of
communicating across a cultural divide.

But there's a definite shift in the second half of the passage as
Forster moves away from dramatic presentation to a more
serious investigation of the situation. Introductions are made,
there is evident good-will on both sides, but the English visitors
cannot bridge the gap between colonisers and colonised. There's
a failure of social formulas; cultural differences are too wide:
the public, unsympathetic exposure too severe for the shy
Indian ladies. Adela's well-intentioned but unsubtle approach to
them seems wonderfully symbolised by the boisterous terrier
that they alternately fondle or avoid. This part of the passage is

marked by small awkwardnesses and indeterminacies – 'cowering', 'recovering', 'giggling', 'fondling' and 'shrinking'. Such 'tiny gestures' fail to connect the two parties, or allow any social momentum to develop. Adela's optimism that the English language can unite people is quickly dashed against 'the echoing walls' of the Indians' 'civility', but she finds that the alternative tactic of saying 'nothing', in its turn, produces 'nothing'.

I would say that this passage introduces us to an important central theme in the novel, namely the yearning for communication and connection that all the major characters share, but also its difficulties – even impossibility – on any lasting basis. The 'Bridge Party' is just the most formal of several such attempts. Some, like the meeting of Aziz and Mrs Moore at the mosque, or Aziz and the subaltern on the Maidan, are lucky unforeseen accidents, and the former has profound consequences that could not be predicted at the time, but others, like Fielding's tea party or Aziz's sick-bed levee, are wrangling, inconsequential affairs that always threaten to break up in frustration. Of course, the visit to the caves is the climax of such efforts and its ominous nature is already prefigured in the 'echoing walls' of the ladies' civility that Adela vainly strives against here. I'd like to move on now and look at Adela's relationship with Ronny which is her attempt to develop a more intimate, private life, and her reason for coming to India.

3   Select a second passage for discussion

'I think we shall keep friends.'
'I know we shall.'
'Quite so.'
As soon as they had exchanged this admission, a wave of relief passed through them both, and then transformed itself into a wave of tenderness, and passed back. They were softened by their own honesty, and began to feel lonely and unwise. Experiences, not character, divided them; they were not dissimilar, as human beings go; indeed, when compared with the people who stood nearest to them in point of space they became practically identical. The Bhil who was holding an officer's polo pony, the Eurasian who drove the Nawab Bahadur's car, the Nawab Bahadur himself, the Nawab Baha-

dur's debauched grandson – none would have examined a
difficulty so frankly and coolly. The mere fact of examination
caused it to diminish. Of course they were friends, and for
ever. 'Do you know what the name of that green bird up above
us is?' she asked, putting her shoulder rather nearer to his.
    'Bee-eater.'
    'Oh, no, Ronny, it has red bars on its wings.'
    'Parrot,' he hazarded.
    'Good gracious no.'
    The bird in question dived into the dome of the tree. It was
of no importance, yet they would have liked to identify it, it
would somehow have solaced their hearts. But nothing in
India is identifiable, the mere asking of a question causes it to
disappear or to merge in something else. (pp. 100–1)

This is a more intimate passage taken from Chapter 8 when
Adela and Ronny are contemplating the end of their relationship. Seeing Ronny in his pompous role as a white sahib has
decided Adela against an engagement. Given this context, it
seems odd that the tension here is not so much between the
estranged pair, but between them and the rest of India. Lonely
foreigners in a strange land, they feel irrationally drawn to each
other at the moment of parting. Not only are they emotionally
confused, but lost in other ways too. The foreign culture that has
driven them apart also makes them feel vulnerable and dependent on each other in a manner that they find difficult to
express. Despite their differences, they seek to maintain their
shared cultural identity in a landscape that they suddenly sense
is alien to them and the values that they share.
    As in the last passage, we have the same mix of dialogue that
borders on comedy and a commentating authorial presence that
strikes a sad, even sombre, tone. The first thing that draws my
attention is the inadequacy of language to express feelings or to
connect people. This links this passage with the first one we
looked at. The young people have been 'awfully British' (p. 100)
in their emotional reticence and self-control but Adela feels
obscurely cheated by this; for some time she has felt the need for
a thorough talk and now there is nothing left to say.
    Paradoxically, the limited, constrained language that has just
parted them also stimulates regret; it reinforces their sense of
being 'awfully British'. No Indian would have examined their

emotional problems 'so frankly and coolly' as they have done. This reconciliation takes the form of an emotional 'wave' of relief and tenderness that passes between them, but this is unspoken and cannot be articulated or openly declared; that would not be 'British'. It does have the effect, however, of bringing them closer together in the unfamiliar world that they suddenly find themselves in and Adela seeks some purchase on. Their sensible rationality may have divided them, but culturally it is a bond when they are faced with an Indian tribesman, a half-cast chauffeur, a Moslem dignitary and his dissolute grandson. These figures are as strange to them, as 'unlabelled', as the unnamed bird. Thus Forster has set out the context where their unsatisfactory relationship seems likely to continue despite Adela's wiser instincts.

This notion of the inadequacies of language is taken up by the failure of the pair to name the little green bird. There is an element of comedy about this – Adela, as ever, naively keen to learn, Ronny reluctant and lazy – but it also takes up a serious point that is developed and elaborated throughout the book. Adela and Ronny are typical Western rationalists in their attempt to 'name', 'label' and so control their experiences and their world. The elusive green bird exposes the futility of this endeavour in the complex, multiform experience of India. It cannot, any more than India itself, be reduced to a simple, knowable meaning. Adela's puzzled inquiry here can be compared with Mrs Moore's untroubled regard of the wasp on the cloak-peg at the end of Chapter 3. The wasp, ignoring the man-made boundaries of outdoor and indoor, nature and society, has chosen the spot for sleep and Mrs Moore accepts it with her benign, Christian charity and blessing of 'pretty dear' (p. 55). This spirit seems more in accord with the confusions of India where 'nothing ... is identifiable, the mere asking of a question causes it to disappear or to merge in something else'.

If the bird is one small example of unknowable India, the unidentified 'hairy beast' that causes the Nawab's car to crash later in this chapter is another. This mystery is more active and malign in that it brings the pair together again despite Adela's better judgement, but both bird and beast anticipate the mysteries and confusions of the Marabar Caves which similarly defeat Adela's rational mind with much more serious and far-reaching consequences.

One last thought I have about the passage concerns Adela's compulsive need to identify and label: it is something of a paradox that tells us much about her character that she needs to label yet dislikes being labelled herself. She is irrationally disappointed later in this chapter when, after the crash, she makes it up with Ronny and finds herself formally engaged almost against her will: 'Unlike the green bird or the hairy animal, she was labelled now' (p. 109). This fear of definitive 'labelling' is expressed again on the journey to the Marabar Caves where she confides to Aziz her fear of becoming 'Anglo-Indian' by marrying Ronny; as she says, 'I can't avoid the label' (p. 157). Language, it seems, can express meanings but it can also constrain and imprison people, things or events, into false or inadequate definitions. Let us move on now to examine a passage from that abortive Marabar expedition.

4   Select a third passage for discussion

Nor had Adela much to say to him. If his mind was with the breakfast, hers was mainly with her marriage. Simla next week, get rid of Antony, a view of Tibet, tiresome wedding bells, Agra in October, see Mrs Moore comfortably off from Bombay – the procession passed before her again, blurred by the heat, and then she turned to the more serious business of her life in Chandrapore. There were real difficulties here – Ronny's limitations and her own – but she enjoyed facing difficulties, and decided that if she could control her peevishness (always her weak point), and neither rail against Anglo-India nor succumb to it, their married life ought to be happy and profitable. She mustn't be too theoretical; she would deal with each problem as it came up, and trust to Ronny's common sense and her own. Luckily, each had abundance of common sense and good will.

But as she toiled over a rock that resembled an inverted saucer, she thought, 'What about love?' The rock was nicked by a double row of footholds, and somehow the question was suggested by them. Where had she seen footholds before? Oh yes, they were the pattern traced in the dust by the wheels of the Nawab Bahadur's car. She and Ronny – no, they did not love each other.

'Do I take you too fast?' inquired Aziz for she had paused, a doubtful expression on her face. The discovery had come so suddenly that she felt like a mountaineer whose rope had broken. Not to love the man one's going to marry! Not to find out till this moment! Not even to have asked oneself the question until now! Something else to think out. Vexed rather than appalled, she stood still, her eyes on the sparkling rock. There was esteem and animal contact at dusk, but the emotion that links them was absent. Ought she to break her engagement off? She was inclined to think not – it would cause so much trouble to others; besides she wasn't convinced that love is necessary to a successful union. If love is everything, few marriages would survive the honeymoon. 'No, I'm all right thanks,' she said, and, her emotion well under control, resumed the climb, though she felt a bit dashed. Aziz held her hand, the guide adhered to the surface like a lizard and scampered about as if governed by a personal centre of gravity. (pp. 162–3)

At this point Adela and Aziz, with their guide, are climbing on alone up the Kawa Dol after leaving Mrs Moore with the rest of the party preparing breakfast. They are both rather bored and uninterested, their minds on other things; Aziz is preoccupied with his social responsibilities and Adela with thoughts of her forthcoming marriage. It is in this mood that Adela suddenly discovers that she doesn't love Ronny. It is a revelation that both the presence of Aziz and the Marabar rocks seem to play a part in. The passage shows a conflict between Adela's surface, rational mind and a deeper dismay that she attempts to conceal and control by her 'common sense'. It is this dangerous gap between her thoughts and feelings that the strange Indian scenery seems to expose. The last passage showed something of her mixed feelings when she attempted to make the break with Ronny; here she is with Aziz, whom she will later accuse of rape. Both episodes reveal aspects of Adela's gathering emotional 'muddle' and her attempts to repress her growing confusion; in both of them she is in close proximity to a young man.

Once again Adela's search for 'the real India' leads her into troubling and confusing discoveries about herself. We can also see the difficulties of communication that have been a feature of earlier passages. In the previous passage Adela found herself linked culturally to Ronny despite herself; here, as in the 'Bridge Party', there is no communication across the racial and cultural divide. Adela will go on to patronise and disconcert Aziz with tactless questions on his marital state which reveal her assumption of racial and cultural superiority while recognising his physical attractiveness. Though these assumptions are not as crude as Mrs Turton's or Ronny's, they still exist, and show the power of cultural imperialism; even the well-intentioned Adela is not exempt from its pervasive influence and so she is right to fear 'labelling' as an 'Anglo-Indian'; whether she rails, or succumbs, married to Ronny, this is what she will inevitably become.

Adela's predictable future, rather like her view of India, unrolls like a frieze before her; Simla, Tibet, Agra, wedding bells, Bombay – these form a superficial 'procession' of 'blurred' events that hold no attraction for her. Even the wedding bells are 'tiresome', a necessary preliminary to the 'serious business' of married life in Chandrapore with its bracing 'difficulties'. As Adela gathers her attention to the reality of marriage, she pluckily resolves to make the most of it in a stoical fashion, but there's something rather jarring in her utilitarian notion that her marriage 'ought to be happy and profitable' if only she could 'control her peevishness'. Peevish is a word that suggests discontent in a fretful, unfulfilled character who is not in complete accord with herself. Adela cautions herself against being 'too theoretical' but that, of course, is exactly what she is. It is in this state of mind that the Marabar rock seems to challenge her and force her to confront the truth.

In the build-up to this scene, the Marabar is shown to be hostile and alien to human scale and human values. Even the guide becomes a scampering lizard adhering to the rock in an unnatural fashion. Toiling up its smooth, bare surface, Adela is exposed and vulnerable; the plainness of the scenery draws her attention to her own emotional barrenness: 'What about love?' By a train of association, the 'nicked' footholds in the rock remind her of the 'nicked lozenges' in the Nawab's car tyres that she saw in the dust after the accident. She had traced the pattern of them there until 'all went mad' (p. 104). On that occasion, a sudden, hostile force had come out of the night to make the car swerve violently; it had also caused a sudden 'swerve' in her relationship with Ronny. In a manner that prefigures the trial scene later, Adela again relives the experience of the 'esteem and animal contact at dusk' in the present blazing heat. 'Eyes on the sparkling rock', she faces up to the truth: 'She and Ronny – no, they did not love each other.' Once again, a dark, unacknowledged force has broken into her life and could cause it to 'swerve' violently.

Forster captures well Adela's momentary panic and loss of equilibrium as she tries to regain her emotional balance. Like the mountaineer 'whose rope had broken' there's a sudden sense of danger and suspension that she corrects by exerting her own 'abundance of common sense'. Her first response is one of irritation and annoyance at not having discovered this before, closely followed by the characteristic attempts at rational analysis she would employ on any problem. What we see here is the intellectual repression of emotional fears: her realisation has become merely 'Something else to think out'. Thoughts of breaking off the engagement are rejected as inconvenient and selfish, while love, she reasons, is not essential to a 'successful union'. In this mood and 'a bit dashed', she resumes her climb to the caves.

The bleak inhospitality of the Marabar is a fit setting for Adela's depressing revelation. For her, its barren stone, smooth like a 'saucer', becomes symbolic of harsh, unyielding truths that must be accepted, and give no solace nor escape. Adela does attempt to repress her discovery for reasons of personal pride and social convenience – and the result is break-down and sexual hysteria. But although Forster has prepared us well for the catastrophe to come by showing us the state of Adela's mind at this point, events seem to have a logic that transcends individual psychology and incorporates the menace of the Indian landscape itself. At this more mysterious, irrational level, the manner in which the 'nicked' footholds activate the memory trace of the car accident is an anticipation of the more violent 'swerve' events are going to take when Adela enters the cave and is taken over by forces she cannot understand or control.

One last point about the style of the passage. There's nothing very innovative about it, but it is a particularly good example of Forster's skilful use of free indirect speech. This is always a characteristic of his style as a novelist and is a technique which enables him to move inside and outside Adela's muddled mind as omniscient narrator, sympathetically identifying with her, but also judging her. We can see this mobility of view point in the way we are drawn outwards to see the shocked pause in her climb, her 'doubtful expression', and then taken back inside the flow of her thoughts for the series of exasperated exclamations that follow. We relive with her the moment of 'animal contact at dusk' and her understanding that the emotion that should link this physical excitement with personal respect has always been lacking. The public reassurance to Aziz – 'I'm all right thanks' – is in her own words, but the internal assessment that her emotions are now 'well under control' is a little more detached, and so we feel more inclined to query it. 'Vexed rather than appalled' has a similar sort of status; the sentiments are hers but the phrasing is Forster's which has the immediate effect of putting them in a wider context and so open to question. 'A bit dashed' returns us to her own idiom and is such a masterly understatement that it draws upon the reader's sympathy for her plight.

I want to move on now to see how Forster treats Adela after the trial when, her 'passage' nearly completed, she is preparing to return to England.

5   Select a fourth passage for discussion

'This false start has been all my own fault. I was bringing to Ronny nothing that ought to be brought, that was why he rejected me really. I entered that cave thinking: Am I fond of him? I have not yet told you that, Mr Fielding. I didn't feel justified. Tenderness, respect, personal intercourse – I tried to make them take the place – of –'

'I no longer want love,' he said, supplying the word.

'No more do I. My experiences here have cured me. But I want others to want it.'

'But to go back to our first talk (for I suppose this is our last one) – when you entered the cave, who did follow you, or did no one follow you? Can you now say? I don't like it left in air.'

'Let us call it the guide,' she said indifferently. 'It will never be known. It's as if I ran my finger along that polished wall in the dark, and cannot get further. I am up against something, and so are you. Mrs Moore – she did know.'

'How could she have known what we don't?'

'Telepathy, possibly.'

The pert meagre word fell to the ground. Telepathy? What an explanation! Better withdraw it, and Adela did so. She was at the end of her spiritual tether, and so was he. Were there worlds beyond which they could never touch, or did all that is possible enter their consciousness? They could not tell. They only realized that their outlook was more or less similar, and found in this a satisfaction. Perhaps life is a mystery, not a muddle; they could not tell. Perhaps the hundred Indias which fuss and squabble so tiresomely are one, and the universe they mirror is one. They had not the apparatus for judging. (pp. 260–1)

This is taken from the end of the 'Caves' section just before Adela leaves India; in the spirit of their new-found friendship, Adela and Fielding seek to evaluate and provide some sort of rational explanation for the cave débâcle before they part. There is a tension between their desire for the truth and the realisation that they will never find it.

Fielding is the curious one here – he doesn't like things 'left in air' – Adela is more chastened and philosophic. While Fielding admits that he is cynical about love, Adela no longer seeks it for herself, 'But I want others to want it'. This shows a new generosity of spirit, and her earlier self-analysis shows that she has now a greater understanding of herself and her needs. To Fielding's insistent questioning of what actually happened in the caves, she can only suggest the guide, but with no conviction that he is the key to the matter. What happened there is a mystery that must be accepted and cannot be explained in terms that she or Fielding could understand. Mrs Moore knew, but rationalists like themselves are 'up against something'. Pseudo-scientific words like 'telepathy' are pathetically inadequate. There seem to be worlds closed to them, like those imprisoned in the polished Marabar reflections that Adela touched but could not reach. She simply could not 'get further'. So once again this passage shows the inadequacy of Western rationalism in the world of a 'hundred Indias', a world of confusing appearances that might be 'muddle' or 'mystery' – 'They had not the apparatus for judging'. The tone of the passage seems to sympathise with these limitations but also rise above them, subsume them in a wider, wiser vision that is more inclusive. Adela and Fielding are shrunk, reduced to this new scale of things – limited by class, education and race, they are at the end of their spiritual tethers – their only consolation the knowledge of shared values. As Forster writes at their parting: 'A friendliness as of dwarfs shaking hands, was in the air' (p. 262).

Whether the universe is a 'muddle' or a 'mystery' has been a dominant question from the beginning of the book. In Chapter 7 at Fielding's tea party, there's a little debate on the matter. Adela says that she 'hates mysteries', Mrs Moore 'likes mysteries' but 'dislikes muddles', while Fielding considers that 'a mystery is only a high-sounding term for a muddle', and that 'India's a muddle' (p. 86). Throughout the novel, India, or the voices of 'the hundred Indias', have been challenging or mocking by turns. It seems clear by this stage in the text that India has become a kind of metaphor for the universe itself, where Man – certainly Western Christian man – is no longer felt to have a privileged place in the world with the ability to confirm meaning, like Adam in the Genesis story who named God's creation. We have been brought to an awareness that much reality escapes language. 'Telepathy', a 'pert, meagre' word, is inadequate to express the mystery of the Marabar Caves, and Mrs Moore's intuitive understanding of what went on there. Following the thread of Adela's 'passage' through India, we seem to have gone beyond her own personal domestic drama, or even a critique of the colonial mentality and the presence of the British in India, to a more inclusive view of all human kind lost in an alien universe that may be a 'muddle' or a 'mystery'.

What strikes me as significant about the passage stylistically is the manner in which it is dominated by negative constructions: 'cannot get further'; 'It will never be known'; 'never touch'; 'could not tell' (twice); 'had not the apparatus for judging'. This sense of insecurity and doubt is shared by characters and narrator alike; the narrator enforces a sense of provisionality and caution with the exclamation 'What an explanation!', and the use of 'better withdraw'; 'perhaps' is used twice, and his own questioning – 'Were there worlds beyond which they could never touch, or did all that is possible enter their consciousness?' – echoes Fielding's on a grander, more cosmic scale.

One last thought. This lack of confidence seems to find additional expression in the structural organisation of the text. The plot motif of a young girl engaged to one man but ending up marrying another is a standard one in mainstream popular fiction. A predictable end to this novel would be Adela's marriage to that nice Mr Fielding. Aziz certainly suspects this turn of events and it would make a neat, reassuring conclusion to the novel. But it is the expected option that Forster rejects. For him, as much as for Adela, conventional marriage represents a falsity: the assumptions about family continuity and social stability that this solution inscribes are far too comfortable for Forster to endorse. Instead the heroine no longer wants love and the heterosexual 'love plot' peters out with the 'Temple' section of the novel still to go. Here, Aziz's friendship with Fielding is brought forward as the dominant human interest, but this too fails to provide a comforting human solution to the text's anxieties about the fallibility of human communication and connection. In the final paragraph the pair are forced to ride apart knowing their lasting friendship is 'not yet . . . not there' (p. 316).

6   Have I achieved a sufficiently complex sense of the novel?

Clearly this is not the case. Even at the level of individual psychology and human relationships, which are the basis for all novels, there is much still to do. We have followed Adela's progress through the novel, but now this needs to be supplemented by an examination of the relationships between Fielding and Aziz, Aziz and Mrs Moore, and Mrs Moore and Ronny, before we can say that we have a grip on the novel in the basic sense of knowing the story and understanding the social issues. Still, though the work I've done is, in some ways, marginal to the novel's key relationships and key events, I'm quite pleased with the progress I've made. I've used Adela's 'passage' as a thread to follow through the political and social elements that are an important element in the fiction, and, in the process, I've become aware of wider, more mysterious concerns that Forster shows about 'muddle', 'mystery', 'meaning', loss of meaning, and our place in the universe.

While you need to go on and examine other relationships in the text to build up your own basic analysis, I want to carry on and examine some of these more metaphysical questions, and Forster's treatment of them, as they are important aspects of the text. This will involve leaving the social basis of the story for an investigation into Forster's distinctive use of symbolism, as well as other techniques he uses to shape his novel that are not reliant on plot. In fact, my focus on Adela's story has made me realise how much of the effect of the novel does not depend on orthodox story-telling in the old-fashioned sense – and how much I've been forced to leave out. There seems to be two different sorts of structure in *A Passage to India*; one that is linear and to do with the telling of a story, and another that is rhythmic and cyclical, and this has little to do with the narrative as such; its purpose is to express the theme of the novel – its message overall. This more subtle form of textual organisation takes longer to pick out because it requires a closer reading and scrupulous attention to the nuances of the language; you really need to 'listen' to the novel, to be alert to its distinctive lyricism and poetry. If you do this, you will soon become aware that there are motifs – key words and phrases – that are repeated and orchestrated, and that expand their meaning in each new context. The organisation of the text into three sections clearly has something to do with this other, less tangible structure, as do certain, rather mysterious characters who are marginal to the main events of the story. I refer, of course, to Mrs Moore and Professor Godbole. These, then, are some of the aspects of the novel that I'm going on to examine in the next section.

II Aspects of the novel

Let us start with a consideration of the Marabar Caves as they are clearly the richest, most ambivalent symbol in the novel as well as the most important physical location for the plot. Much has been written about them by the critics, and you are in danger of getting hopelessly confused if you try and understand it all at once. It is a better tactic to read what Forster actually writes and try to form your own judgement on their significance before you get too carried away by other people's ideas. I can only indicate some possibilities here, but they are only possibilities, open to challenge and development.

I said at the end of the last section that there seem to be two different sorts of structure in this novel. One that is narrative and another that is less tangible, more poetic. Clearly the caves are vital to them both. On the narrative level something – or nothing – happened to Adela in one of them that is crucial to the plot; it is the turning point for all subsequent events. In an important later interview in 1952 (partly reprinted in the *Macmillan Casebook* on *A Passage to India*), Forster made the much quoted observation that the caves 'were something to focus everything up': they were 'a cavity' which the characters had to pass through, and were 'to engender an event like an egg'. At a more poetic, suggestive level, Mrs Moore's experience in the caves is equally important though its impact on the plot is more diffuse and difficult to assess.

Principally it lies in her spiritual decline and refusal to attend the trial as a witness for the defence. Our sense of the caves, then, is of something overwhelmingly menacing and sinister. The threatening 'fists and fingers' (p. 139) of the Marabar Hills are ominously present from the opening chapter onwards, and during the fateful expedition to see the caves their whole environment is described in very negative terms. However, one important question that we do have to ask ourselves is: are they actively evil, or do they merely amplify whatever human moods and emotions that are brought into them? What exactly *is* their nature? Let us try to draw together some initial ideas to help with this complex problem by looking at the manner in which Forster describes them in the opening chapter to the 'Caves' section of the novel.

> They are dark caves. Even when they open towards the sun, very little light penetrates down the entrance tunnel into the circular chamber. There is little to see, and no eye to see it, until the visitor arrives for his five minutes, and strikes a match. Immediately another flame rises in the depths of the rock and moves towards the surface like an imprisoned spirit: the walls of the circular chambers have been most marvellously polished. The two flames approach and strive to unit, but cannot, because one of them breathes air, the other stone. A mirror inlaid with lovely colours divides the lovers, delicate stars of pink and grey interpose, exquisite nebulae, shadings fainter than the tail of a comet or the midday moon, all the evanescent life of the granite, only here visible. Fists and fingers thrust above the advancing soil – here at last is their skin, finer than any covering acquired by the animals,

smoother than windless water, more voluptuous than love. The radiance increases, the flames touch one another, kiss, expire. The cave is dark again, like all the caves. (pp. 138–9)

We must be alert to the dangers of making too selective a reading from small passages, and remind ourselves of the context from which this paragraph comes. The whole of Chapter 12 stresses the incredible age of the caves; the Marabar Hills are part of the oldest rock on earth – they were there before anything else, historical or prehistorical. The manner in which Forster writes of them gives them an extraordinary presence and significance. 'Older than all spirit' they function as a kind of primeval blank page. They contain nothing and represent nothing, yet paradoxically this is what makes them extraordinary.

They are 'dark caves' and so resistant to the power of the sun which Forster suggests is all-powerful elsewhere in India. No natural light can enter them. They are dependent on a transitory human agency to give them light and reveal their amazing beauty. The paragraph I've chosen is taken up by a description of a visitor's flame and its reflection in the rock.

The Marabar Hills are menacing when viewed from the outside, their 'Fists and fingers thrust above the advancing soil', but their skin, normally thought of as an outside covering, can only be discovered by going inside the caves which is a strange, rather disorientating reversal. This skin is extraordinarily delicate; the narrator emphasises its sensuousness which exceeds all other things whether they be living (finer than any animals), natural ('smoother than windless water'), or ideal ('more voluptuous than love'). The effect of all this is to make the rock the most sensate of things instead of the most dead and inert.

In the opening chapter of the novel, the structural counterpart to this one that introduces the 'Mosque' section, Forster stresses the power of the 'overarching sky' that expands, in ever-widening circles, away from the earth throughout the universe (p. 32). It is a key idea that is taken up repeatedly in the first section. At the beginning of the 'Bridge Party' in Chapter 5, for example, Forster writes: 'Beyond the sky must not there be something that overarches all the skies, more impartial even than they? Beyond which again ... ' (p. 60). The effect of the passage we are looking at here is to achieve a strange reversal of this idea. Once illuminated, the polished surface of the cave reveals hidden depths that seem, in an enclosed, transitory, 'evanescent' way, to contain all the beauty of the universe – comets, moons, stars and nebulae. In the caves, the cosmos is turned inside out, concentrated and reduced in scale. This is a powerful, imaginative notion. Instead of being encouraged to expand our minds ever outwards as we are in the 'Mosque' section, here we are sucked inwards into a vortex or infinite regress.

However, the match's illumination of the beautiful surface of the rock is almost an incidental by-product of its true intention which is to unite with the other flame that its presence invokes. Caught in the rock 'like an imprisoned spirit' this other flame rises to meet it. 'The two flames . . . strive to unite' but although similar are of different elements. Forster is at pains to suggest the independent nature of the rock flame – breathing rock rather than air, it seems more than a passive reflection – but the flames are destined never to unite and become one: they can only touch, kiss and die in mutual extinction. The effect of this is mysterious, erotic, beautiful and sad. It is suggestive of the doomed nature of human love and supports the idea that human beings are inevitably solitary and locked into themselves. Never able to do more than reach out for each other, the very touch of erotic fulfilment is sufficient to extinguish their desire. Such a notion ties in with the yearning for human connection at all levels that is such a pervasive theme in the novel, a yearning that emotion demands, but reason denies. Remember the baffled frustration of Adela who 'ran' her 'finger along that polished wall' (p. 260) of the cave but could not 'get further'. It is worth pointing out, however, that it is only through the illumination of the flame that the wonderful world of the stone becomes visible.

But what about the caves themselves? I still may not be very sure what they signify, it is in the nature of symbols to be open to differing readings and interpretations, but it is difficult to think of them as simply evil after studying such an intense, lyrical passage; so much imaginative force has been invested in them. Here at least, they seem to be a place of mystery and poetic 'presence' rather than being merely negative and destructive, though we should add that this poetry has been brought in from outside by the narrator. They may contain nothing but nothing has been made into something by the presence and reflection of the flame, a something that though transitory, maybe even illusionary, is still registered as beautiful by the human narrative voice experiencing and recording it.

I shall be returning to examine another aspect of the caves later but before I do that I want to look at a passage from the first section of the novel. If the caves are primeval and untouched by human agency, 'Mosque' clearly indicates something quite different. A mosque is an expression in architecture of a recognisable human aspiration, culturally and historically specific. Aziz's dreams of an Islamic world of poetry and justice. His idealisation of the rule of the Mogul emperors in India, and his yearnings for the 'ideal friend', dominate the first section, and contrast ironically with the reality of the British Raj. Other motifs include the predominance of evening scenes and the beauties of India at night under a strong Oriental moon, for, as Forster has noted, the opening of the novel is set in the Indian winter before the onset of the great summer heat. The choice of this season allows Forster to celebrate the lyrical possibilities of India outside Aziz's imaginative dream-world as well as within it.

You can see all these elements in the first meeting between Aziz and Mrs Moore in Chapter 2. It is a scene that I would recommend you to examine closely for it is here, despite all the obvious barriers of age, sex, class, religion and race, that two human beings do manage to reach out and 'touch' each other in a meaningful and lasting way that lies outside the normal pattern of human relationships. The fact that this fateful meeting takes place in a mosque must have some significance for the naming of this section. 'Mosque' in this context seems to suggest those brief, special moments where we glimpse the possibilities of friendship and love: what Forster calls 'the secret understanding of the heart' (p. 42). I want to extend the debate beyond the personal, though, by looking at the end of Chapter 7, which describes the breaking-up of Fielding's tea party.

> 'Good-bye, Mr Fielding, and thank you so much . . . What lovely College buildings!'
> 'Good-bye, Mrs Moore.'
> 'Good-bye, Mr Fielding. Such an interesting afternoon . . .'
> 'Good-bye, Miss Quested.'
> 'Good-bye, Dr Aziz.'

'Good-bye, Mrs Moore.'

'Good-bye, Dr Aziz.'

'Good-bye, Miss Quested.' He pumped her hand up and down to show that he felt at ease. 'You'll jolly jolly well not forget those caves, won't you? I'll fix the whole show up in a jiffy.'

'Thank-you . . .'

Inspired by the devil to a final effort, he added, 'What a shame you leave India so soon! Oh! do reconsider your decision, do stay.'

'Good-bye, Professor Godbole,' she continued, suddenly agitated. 'It's a shame we never heard you sing.'

'I may sing now,' he replied, and did.

His thin voice rose, and gave out one sound after another. At times there seemed rhythm, at times there was the illusion of a Western melody. But the ear, baffled repeatedly, soon lost any clue, and wandered in a maze of noises, none harsh or unpleasant, none intelligible. It was the song of an unknown bird. Only the servants understood it. They began to whisper to one another. The man who was gathering water chestnuts came naked out of the tank, his lips parted with delight, disclosing his scarlet tongue. The sounds continued and ceased after a few moments as casually as they had begun – apparently half through a bar, and upon the subdominant.

'Thanks so much: what was that?' asked Fielding.

'I will explain in detail. It was a religious song. I placed myself in the position of a milkmaiden. I say to Shri Krishna, "Come! come to me only." The god refuses to come. I grow humble and say: "Do not come to me only. Multiply yourself into a hundred Krishnas, and let one go to each of my hundred companions, but one, O Lord of the Universe, come to me." He refuses to come. This is repeated several times. The song is composed in a raga appropriate to the present hour, which is the evening.'

'But he comes in some other song, I hope?' said Mrs Moore gently.

'Oh, no, he refuses to come,' repeated Godbole, perhaps not understanding her question. 'I say to him, "Come, come, come, come, come, come." He neglects to come.'

Ronny's steps had died away, and there was a moment of absolute silence. No ripple disturbed the water, no leaf stirred. (pp. 95–6)

Let's begin by placing the passage in its narrative sequence. Learning that Mrs Moore has met and liked Aziz and that Adela wants to see 'the real India', Fielding invites them both to tea at the Government College. Aziz and Professor Godbole are also invited. This chapter then is just part of a sequence of invitations attempting to bridge racial and cultural divisions. 'Mosque' consists largely of such meetings and attempts at connection – in the mosque itself, the Club gardens, the Maidan, around Aziz's sick-bed, and here in Fielding's garden house, which is appropriately Islamic in architecture. The party is a mixture of races and creeds: European and Indian, Christian, Moslem and Hindu. At first things go well; Fielding and Aziz quickly become intimate, and, encouraged by the architecture and informal atmosphere, Aziz becomes expansive in his dreams of Mogul hospitality. It is in this mood that he invites the two English women to visit the caves. However, all is spoilt by the arrival of Ronny; the party breaks up in disorder under his official, disapproving eye.

This passage opens with the sad good-byes of social parting and social defeat. Aziz, uncomfortable and ill at ease, assumes a familiarity he does not feel and insists on an invitation that he does not want to give. The jarring jocularity of his speech, the clumsy misplaced slang, the over-vigorous hand-shake, dramatise all this very well. This social unease intensifies into real embarrassment when he inadvertently reveals to Ronny that Adela has decided to leave India before he has been told it himself. Then Forster goes through one of his characteristic sudden turns, a quick shift of tone and mood into something much more expansive and mysterious.

Unexpectedly, and oddly tangential to the narrative sequence that the 'good-byes' seem to be directing us towards, Godbole decides to sing. What he sings is another kind of invitation, this time not to fellow human beings, but to Krishna, the divine 'Lord of the Universe'. The effect of Godbole's apparent eccentricity is to make space for yet one more appeal for touch and connection but one that cuts across personal and social confusions, suddenly placing them into a wider perspective by moving into a different order of reality.

Godbole's raga is a 'muddle' to Western ears. Another example of the confusions of India – 'a maze of noises, none harsh or unpleasant, none intelligible' where the 'baffled' hearer is soon lost – it seems to end as inconclusively and suddenly as it began, with no recognisable harmony. But what is expressed as an inconclusive muddle by the narrator is a keenly appreciated delight to the servants in Fielding's garden. What is closed to us, the readers, is registered in the response of the water chestnut gatherer emerging naked from the tank, 'his lips parted with delight'. Once again India challenges the limitations of an exclusively European view of the world.

The effect of the passage is haunting but very difficult to analyse; there are many such passages in this text that seem to work in the margins or interstices of the plot, and any thorough examination of *A Passage to India* must try to come to terms with them. They are what makes a reading of the novel not unlike the experience of the Godbole song here, 'a maze of noises, none harsh or unpleasant, none intelligible'. One could loosely call such a passage 'atmosphere' or refer to it vaguely as the use of India for poetic background, but that wouldn't be sufficient. It seems too much a part of Forster's narrative strategy for that. I would say that this passage has similarities with the last one we looked at in that, like the flame's frustrated relationship with its stone counterpart, Godbole's rejected, repeated appeal to 'Come, come, come, come, come, come', is both a failure and a kind of success. Godbole seems quite resigned that Krishna 'neglects to come' though we cannot be sure that he understands Mrs Moore's anxious inquiry that he comes 'in some other song, I hope?'.

The passage achieves much of its mysterious force through a tension between absence and presence, where absence becomes a kind of presence. At least this is how I can best explain the strange effect of the final paragraph. Ronny's departing footsteps leave an 'absolute' silence without ripple or stirring leaf, an emptiness that is curiously full of meaning. An expectant space waiting to be filled. Of course, you could say that this emptiness is just a blankness meaning nothing but what I choose to read into it, and it is just this fundamental ambiguity that gives the passage its power.

Godbole is a Hindu of the priestly Brahman caste. His presence in the text is always enigmatic and his statements have a cryptic significance. His equanimity here is best explained by something he says much later in Chapter 19, after the disaster in the caves. Discussing the nature of evil and good, he tells Fielding that 'absence implies presence, absence is not non-existence, and therefore we are entitled to repeat, "Come, come, come, come" ' (p. 186). Such a mystical way of thinking is alien to both Moslem and Christian thought, for these religions are concerned with God as an authenticating power, a 'presence' granting meaning, individuality and exclusivity. For Aziz, like all faithful Moslems, 'there is no God but God' (p. 272) and his ninety-nine attributes are written, black against white, in the marbled mosque. When Mrs Moore meets Aziz there, she is confident that 'God is here' (p. 42). Small wonder then that she is worried at Krishna's failure to come. Her religion depends on simple-minded certainties. As she tells Ronny in Chapter 5, rebuking his colonial arrogance, 'God is love'. India, however, has the capacity to test and undermine such certainties, as the text amply demonstrates. The narrator goes on to tell us that 'God' had been constantly in Mrs Moore's thoughts since being in India, 'though oddly enough he satisfied her less' and she had never found pronouncing his name 'less efficacious' (p. 71).

With these thoughts about religion, meaning, 'presence' and power in mind, I want to return to the Marabar Caves and examine Mrs Moore's negative experience in them.

> She took out her writing pad, and began, 'Dear Stella, Dear Ralph,' then stopped, and looked at the queer valley and their feeble invasion of it. Even the elephant had become a nobody. Her eye rose from it to the entrance tunnel. No, she did not wish to repeat that experience. The more she thought over it, the more disagreeable and frightening it became. She minded it much more now than at the time. The crush and smells she could forget, but the echo began in some indescribable way to undermine her hold on life. Coming at a moment when she chanced to be fatigued, it had managed to murmur, 'Pathos, pity, courage – they exist, but are identical, and so is filth. Everything exists, nothing has value.' If one had spoken vileness in that place, or quoted lofty poetry, the comment would have been the same – 'ou-boum'. (p. 160)

The sinister echo in the caves, and Mrs Moore's reaction to it, has generally been recognised as a climax – a focal point – of some kind. Keeping our minds on the notion of two kinds of structure in the novel, narrative and what I've chosen to call, rather loosely, 'poetic', if Adela's retraction of her charge during the trial is the climax of the first, this seems to be the climax of the second. In fact, as we never know what happens to Adela in her cave, there is really a gap in the narrative at this point, but it also functions as the centre of the novel. All this is very teasing, unsettling and paradoxical. It is as if the whole text is gathered around a hole, an empty space, which we would like to fill with some kind of meaning and significance, but can't. The reader is left in the same position as Mrs Moore herself.

Mrs Moore, we remember, 'liked mysteries' but 'rather disliked muddles' (p. 86), and there is nothing but 'muddle' on a cosmic scale in the Marabar Caves. 'Everything exists, nothing has value.' The bland empty syllable 'ou-boum', apart from duplicating itself into its mirror image of 'bou-oum', reduces the distinction and meaning out of everything: pathos, pity, courage, filth, vileness, poetry. It all sounds the same, with the suggestion that it *is* all the same. Mrs Moore's 'poor little talkative Christianity' (p. 161) cannot absorb and counter such radical nihilism, consequently the echo begins to 'undermine her hold on life'. The elephant, Ralph and Stella may 'exist' but they no longer have 'value'.

So not only do the caves resist meaning themselves, but their echo casts doubt on our capacity to 'label' anything and make proper sense of it. Above all, the echo represents a challenge to language for it is through language that we make meanings, and the echo undermines those distinctions upon which meaning depends. It is only when Mrs Moore begins to write her letter home that the full horror of the cave's message descends on her. At the level of narrative, the caves are an ordeal that the characters have to undergo – they concentrate the action and precipitate dramatic events; in another sense, their echo is an expansive symbol, reverberating ever outwards through the text, not only through the minds of the two women but the reader's as well, undermining, shifting, disturbing fixed positions, making for uncertainty and doubt. Indeed, the challenge of the echo extends to all those systems of thought and faith that we use in our attempts to compel some meaning and order out of a universe that may be quite alien and indifferent to us. The caves refuse to be 'labelled' but do provide a focus and metaphorical access to this frightening thought. That is why they are so disturbing.

All this sounds very pessimistic, but it is interesting to see how

Forster works in the spaces that he has created by his own radical questioning and scepticism to find hope as well as despair. There are certainly pessimistic echoes in the text; Adela has to be exorcised from hers during the trial, Mrs Moore dies still recovering from her disillusion, there are evil consequences from the cave expedition for the inhabitants of Chandrapore generally – but there are optimistic ones too. As we saw with Godbole's song, absence can imply a kind of presence, 'nothing' can become 'something'. Mrs Moore's simple Christian faith is destroyed by the echo, but, in death, she becomes a kind of beneficent echo of herself in the Hindu chant of 'Esmiss Esmoor' that intercedes at the trial. Her simple declaration of 'God is love' makes a reappearance at the Mau festival comically realigned to 'God si love'. Aziz finds himself repeating his accepting phrase to her – 'then you are an Oriental' (p. 45) – to her son Ralph (p. 306), who exerts a kind of 'echo' or replication of her kindly influence at the end of the book. It seems, then, that the negative vision of the Marabar Caves is not final, but part of a process that must be gone through. The text is full of echoes; some do destroy, but there are others that heal.

We are still left with a question: how can Forster impose some sort of meaningful shape on a novel that is always threatening to fall apart into meaninglessness? I'd like to try and answer this by looking finally at a passage from 'Temple', the third section of the novel.

In the courtyard, drenched by the rain, the small Europeanized band stumbled off into a waltz. 'Nights of Gladness' they were playing. The singers were not perturbed by this rival, they live beyond competition. It was long before the tiny fragments of Professor Godbole that attended to outside things decided that his pince-nez was in trouble, and that until it was adjusted he could not choose a new hymn. He laid down one cymbal, with the other he clashed the air, with his free hand he fumbled at the flowers round his neck. A colleague assisted him. Singing into one another's grey moustaches, they disentangled the chain from the tinsel into which it had sunk. Godbole consulted the music-book, said a word to the drummer, who broke rhythm, made a thick little blur of sound, and produced a new rhythm. This was more exciting, the inner images it evoked more definite, and the singers' expressions became fatuous and languid. They loved all men, the whole universe, and the scraps of their past, tiny splinters of detail, emerged for a moment to melt into the universal warmth. Thus Godbole, though she was not important to him, remembered an old woman he had met in Chandrapore days. Chance brought her into his mind while it was in this heated state, he did not select her, she happened to occur among the throng of soliciting images, a tiny splinter, and he impelled her by this spiritual force to that place where completeness can be found. Completeness, not reconstruction. His senses grew thinner, he remembered a wasp seen he forgot where, perhaps on a stone. He loved the wasp equally, he impelled it likewise, he was imitating God. And the stone where the wasp clung – could he . . . no, he could not, he had been wrong to attempt the stone, logic and conscious effort had seduced, he came back to the strip of carpet and discovered that he was dancing upon it. (pp.283–4)

'Temple' is another architectural image of human worship like 'Mosque' and the whole section is taken up with a description of the Hindu festival of Gokul Ashtami. It represents one more attempt to reach out and make meaning through connection with the infinite. But this time not through exclusivity and order as the Moslem and Christian faiths try to do; instead the scene is one of benign chaos, inclusive and accepting of all. Actual architectural details are not dwelt on like the domes and arches of 'Mosque'; the emphasis here is on the human content and contact – a miscellaneous confusion of people, objects, music, dance, noise, expectation, excitement, all outside in the rain, as the community awaits the birth of Krishna. It is a collective experience quite unlike Aziz's private dreams of harmony in an 'eternal garden'.

This is a difficult passage and not untypical of much of the writing in the 'Temple' section as a whole; the initial impression we get is one of complete 'muddle' and comic disarray. The European band playing 'Nights of Gladness' competes incompetently with the Hindu choir, and the priests' antics as they dance appear ridiculous. Godbole himself is an absurd figure without any dignity, jigging about with his pince-nez caught in his garland, clashing his cymbal with the empty air as he attempts to choose another hymn. As Forster describes it, there seems to be no form or meaning in the ritual, just a great jumble of unconnected images. But out of all this disorder comes meaning and order of a kind, both for the participants in the ritual and the reader of the novel. Reason, logic, conscious effort are temporarily suspended in the mystic dance which becomes an image of ecstatic completeness, of physical, mental and spiritual harmony that lies outside time and time's demands. As the singers grow 'fatuous and languid' in their musically induced trance, so they seek to love all things and 'melt into the universal warmth'.

Godbole attends to the tiny 'splinters of detail', fragments of memory that come unbidden into his consciousness; he wishes, like God, to love them all equally and, by doing so, invest them with fresh meaning and a renewed existence. As we are drawn into his mind so we too can experience these 'soliciting' images, and how Godbole seeks to impel them into a place 'where completeness can be found'. These 'scraps' from the past turn out to be Mrs Moore, a wasp and a stone – a motley trio that, like everything else in the passage, seem to have no relationship with each other. Godbole believes himself successful in his attempts to accept and love Mrs Moore and the wasp equally, so aspiring to God-like charity, but he fails with the stone. And failing, he is drawn back to time and place: the red carpet and himself 'dancing upon it'.

What is the significance of all this and its meaning for the novel as a whole? I think we can begin to see a pattern if we look back to other passages that we have examined in this section. As we've noted, Godbole's trance, like the festival of which it is a part, is just one more attempt to reach out from the constraints of our humanity and touch something grander and more impersonal than ourselves, another effort to find meaning outside the trivial concerns of our day-to-day lives. In his efforts to transcend his individuality and become one with God, Godbole is akin to the frustrated Marabar flame that briefly 'kisses' the polished surface of the caves, illuminates its marvels and then expires.

At Fielding's tea party, Godbole called to Krishna in the guise of a milkmaiden and, much to Mrs Moore's distress, he 'neglects to come'. Here, finally, at the ceremony of his birth, he does appear to 'come'; for a few precious moments he transcends time and space to make himself manifest in the rapt expressions and behaviour of his followers. Above all, the exhilarating 'muddle' and confusion of the Mau festival seems to provide some sort of answer to the desolating echo of the Marabar Caves. In the Marabar, all human effort to signify, to make meaning, was frustrated. Everything was reduced to nothing. Here, some sort of strange reversal takes place. Everything is equal, and equally significant. 'Muddle' becomes mysterious; indeed 'muddle' is seen to be an essential part of 'mystery'.

It seems a deliberate paradox that Mrs Moore should be present when Krishna is absent at Fielding's tea party, but that now, in death and absent herself, her memory should make her present at Krishna's birth. What are we to make of her appearance here in Godbole's mind along with the other random 'soliciting images' of wasp and stone? Well, of course, they are seen as random by Godbole, but they are not that random in the mind of the careful reader, who is able to make connections between them that Godbole cannot make. This is all part of the pleasure of reading the text and making meanings out of it. In his 1952 interview, Forster said that the last section was 'architecturally necessary'; the book 'needed a lump, or Hindu temple if you like – a mountain standing up. It is well placed; and it gathers up some strings'. Clearly Mrs Moore, the wasp and the stone are some of those 'strings'.

If you go back and read carefully, I think you will find that all three play a significant part in the on-going construction of the text and each has a relationship to the others. As a 'character', Mrs Moore's role in the story is manifold and complex, but her relationship with the wasp is particularly interesting. The wasp is a small but significant item in the 'Mosque' section. It plays its part in the theme of invitations and appeals to higher authority that are the substance of that section by being used as a touchstone, both to measure the extent of Mrs Moore's instinctive reverence for life and the inadequacy of conventional Christian theology.

As we saw earlier, Mrs Moore resists the normal tendency of the British to label, define and so control all that they experience in India. She can accept the wasp in her bedroom as a 'pretty dear' (p. 55). At the end of Chapter 4, however, young Mr Sorley becomes uneasy at the thought that wasps might have their share in heavenly bliss: 'we must exclude someone from our gathering, or we shall be left with nothing' (p. 58). The implications of Forster's irony are clear; the wasp is excluded from the conventional Christian heaven but, through Godbole, finds a place in the birth of Krishna. It too finds a 'passage' to more than itself. Of the three religions that feature in the novel, Hinduism is seen to be the most spiritually generous and the one most capable of embracing the muddle of life and drawing significance out of it.

But the stone remains. Man is not God, though he aspires towards that state, and the stone measures the limit of his spiritual capacities, the nature of human incompleteness. Mrs Moore was unable to accept the Marabar and its message destroyed her. Godbole is spiritually stronger, but he cannot love the stone equally; like the Marabar Caves, it remains obdurately outside human understanding and charity. It forces upon him an awareness of human limitation and brings him, quite literally, back to earth.

I think we are in a better position now to see why the novel takes the form that it does, and why the 'Temple' section is essential even though it does little to forward the story. The classic nineteenth-century novel was a dramatic narrative, primarily social in its interests; it worked around the conflict between individual needs and society's demands. The novelist created narrative interest through this conflict which then had to be smoothed away in a tidy, satisfying ending. *A Passage to India* still has this residual pattern in its narrative as we saw when examining Adela's role in the novel. Adela's rather naive desire to see 'the real India' and her disruptive progress through the novel, provide the focus for a strong political and social critique of Western Imperialism. But Forster adds a quite new dimension to the fiction by asking a disturbing, modern question. How is one to achieve a sense of meaning in a meaningless world? Clearly, in this sense, 'India' becomes a modern state of mind as much as a geographical place; it unsettles the reader quite as much as the protagonists in Forster's novel. Traditionally, we have always found meaning in our lives through our relationships with others, the physical world, or God. As we've seen, all of these are tested and found wanting in *A Passage to India*. Is the world a muddle or a mystery? That is the final challenge of the novel.

Forster's solution is to leave the question open. For this he needs an ending that is similarly open without being simply inconclusive. 'Temple' is full of images and scenes of hopeful but temporary reconciliation as God passes briefly through the chaos of human affairs; these reach a crescendo in the drama of the capsizing boats carrying Aziz and Fielding at the climax of the festival. What I have been doing with this passage should show you how Forster uses the 'Temple' section to 'gather up some strings' in the text. It is a good example of how he picks up dominant motifs – images, words, phrases – and weaves them together in a manner that encourages us to draw significances, make meanings, from them, but always to leave us with a sense of openness and provisionality. He never bosses or bullies the reader. In this respect, Godbole becomes a kind of image of Forster himself. Just as Godbole attempts to keep himself open and accepting of all things, so too does the novelist. In the final analysis, Godbole's divine possession and mystic dance become a kind of analogy of the art of writing itself as the novelist reaches out to all that is not himself and makes a passage 'to more than India'.

8
Writing a Forster Essay

There is no one 'correct' way to write on any novelist but an essay must be purposeful and have a recognisable structure. It isn't just 'chat' in writing, however intelligent and informed that might be, but a form of expression that has its own conventions and procedures. The bad news is that these have to be practised and mastered; the good news is that this can be done quite easily. With application and care, it is perfectly possible for everyone to write a good essay, and get a lot of satisfaction in doing so.

Two common problems when writing about a novel

Studying novels is often more fun than studying plays and poems because fiction is so much more like life, but this brings its own dangers when you have to write an essay. There are two temptations in particular which you must try to avoid when writing about any novelist. Firstly, don't simply retell the story without doing anything with it. The reader or examiner presumably knows the story and won't be interested in your version unless it is directed towards some other purpose or point that you wish to make. Secondly, don't simply 'gossip' about characters as if they were real people. There is an acceptable convention of discussing characters in fiction as if they are real – indeed I've used it myself in this book – but it is only a convention, or kind of short-hand, to speed up discussion. It's easy to forget that characters are made out of words and when we talk about a character we are, in fact, talking about a particular artistic strategy within a text that doesn't live an independent life outside it. You need to keep reminding yourself of this fact and always keep your discussion of characters within the context of the fiction – and the function and purpose that any character is intended to fulfil overall. As you are going to write about the story and characters in almost any essay on a novelist, these are common pitfalls because they lead to irrelevance and so weaken many essays. They make it harder to write really well on a novelist, although you may have studied hard and enjoyed the book, so watch out and try to avoid them!

Tackling the question

Here is a typical question that you might be asked on *A Passage to India*:

> Discuss Forster's characterisation of Aziz and consider the role that he plays in *A Passage to India*.

The obvious response to this sort of question is to see the word 'Aziz' and then go straight into your answer, writing down everything you can think of about Aziz, what he is like, the things that he does in the novel and what happens to him. You just follow the narrative of the novel from the first scene until the last – or, if it is an exam, until you run out of time. This is not likely to produce a very good essay, even though you can show that you know the book very well. It won't be a good essay because it is a shapeless sequence of facts without discussion or interpretation. The first thing you must do before starting any essay is read the question carefully and think about its implications. This may be common, standard advice, but it doesn't stop it being ignored on many occasions. You need to break the question down a bit; pick out the key words and note the structure of its phrasing. You need to 'get hold' of it and seek out the possibilities that it offers you. Above all, you must ask yourself: 'what does this question want? What is it looking for?' Sometimes a question has certain assumptions that you might want to argue with.

In this case the question does seem fairly straightforward but it still needs careful consideration. Note that it asks you to discuss 'characterisation' not 'character'; in other words the emphasis has been put on Forster's method of creating Aziz and not simply on Aziz as an individual. The question has been phrased this way to help you remember that 'Aziz' is a constructed fictional entity and not a person. The other important thing to note is that the question falls into two halves. You are asked to discuss Aziz's characterisation, and then to consider the role that he plays in the novel overall. It is vital that you spot this and understand its significance, otherwise you will spend too much of your time writing about Aziz as a person and neglect the second part of the question or ignore it altogether. But this second part is equally important, and the question has been put in this way to make you show a different kind of knowledge. Essay questions rarely ask one simple thing; they can usually be broken down into constituent parts or fall into either/or type antitheses. Good essays must take on the full implications of the question that has been set.

Constructing your answer

The first golden rule is start thinking about the essay that you have to write, rather than the one you would like to write. You may have many more interesting ideas on Fielding or Mrs Moore but it's no good trying to twist an essay title into a more accommodating form. Think about the implications of the question in the way that I've suggested, and then the next step is to sketch out a plan. It shouldn't be very detailed or take very long; a few words or phrases in some kind of sequence is quite sufficient. It doesn't matter how sophisticated or advanced you are in your studies, the second golden rule applies: every essay must have a beginning, middle and end. Hopefully, a plan will force you to think about structuring your essay in this way. It is helpful to have some sense of where you are going before you start, even if you keep some of your options open as to the exact route. Think of it as a provisional guide rather than something that then has to be slavishly followed.

The next step is the hardest and the most crucial: you have to write your opening paragraph. A good opening paragraph is so important because it will determine the rest of the essay. If you start in an irrelevant way, the chances are you will never recover,

or waste a lot of time steering your essay round to the real issues.
Let's think about the question on Aziz that I've been using as an
example. You could well begin by simply stating that Aziz is the
most important character in the novel, and go on from there.
This wouldn't be wrong, but it could easily lead to the kind of
general, uncritical answer that neglects the second part of the
question. A more thoughtful and discriminating opening paragraph might read something like this:

> Aziz is perhaps the most interesting and sympathetic charac-
> ter in Forster's novel. His inner development is traced with
> greater detail than that given to any of the European charac-
> ters. Even Fielding, the character closest to Forster in his
> attitudes, does not receive the attention that Aziz gets. Much
> of the action of the novel revolves around Aziz as well as the
> themes of the novel. We might even say that the success of the
> book depends upon how convincingly he is portrayed, and
> how far Forster succeeds in creating his role as an idealistic
> Indian Moslem.

In starting out in this way I have not committed myself by saying
that Aziz is the most successful character – that's for me to prove
or disprove as the essay develops – but I've made it clear that,
structurally, he is the most important, and suggested some of the
difficulties that he presents. Should I wish to, I've also opened
the way to discussing other characters that contrast with Aziz,
and, most important of all, I've shown that I'm aware and
thinking about the second half of the question before I set off on
the first. The chances of writing a balanced, discerning essay are
greatly improved by an opening paragraph that maps out the
options and notes the problems in this way.

The next step is to build up your essay, paragraph by
paragraph. Make each one carry a fresh idea and show a clear
progression in your argument. For this question you might
select three or four well-spaced episodes from the whole range
that are available to illustrate the complexity of Aziz's characterisation, rather like I did with Adela in my chapter on the novel.
Whether you choose to examine Aziz's behaviour with his fellow
Indians, his colonial rulers, his English friends, or his more
intimate moments when he is by himself, each change of focus
will require a new paragraph and this part of your essay needs

some sort of interim summary underlining what you have shown; you may conclude that Aziz is a triumph of sympathetic identification on Forster's part, or you may have a more measured response and say that he is a character created out of Forster's limitations and strengths as a liberal novelist writing at this time. You could say that Forster cares about Aziz but, as a European writing about an Indian, he also rather patronises him. Aziz doesn't altogether escape the Western stereotype of the Oriental as a charming fellow, but a bit shifty and unreliable when contrasted with, say, Fielding. The point is that it doesn't matter what conclusion you have come to, provided you have amassed enough evidence to make it convincing.

Now you need to switch direction in order to answer the second part of the question. As this asks you to go on and discuss Aziz's 'role' in the novel as a whole, you need to broaden your discussion to include plot and themes. You could point out that the novel operates on several levels; it exposes the evils of colonialism, it makes an impassioned plea for good personal relationships as the most important thing in life, and it also suggests that the universe is a mysterious place where it is difficult for human beings to find security and an abiding home. At this level the novel is more symbolic and metaphysical. Again you must build up your answer, paragraph by paragraph, by showing how Aziz has an important central role in each of these levels of the fiction. You could discuss his treatment by the Anglo-Indian community, his friendship with Fielding, and the more mysterious relationship that he has with Mrs Moore.

Finally, you need a concluding paragraph that takes some sort of overview of the work you have done and relates it back to your opening paragraph. It needn't be very long or elaborate, but it does establish that you have maintained control of your material and never lost sight of the question. You might conclude that Aziz's somewhat ambiguous characterisation is essential for Forster's solution to the formidable problems that the novel expresses as a whole. Colonialism is shown to be an evil in India, and Aziz is damaged by his contact with the English. Yet at a personal level, his life is enriched by his friendship with Fielding and finally redeemed by his memories of Mrs Moore. It is through Aziz, then, that Forster maintains his rather contradictory view of Empire; it is seen as a necessary evil – after all, Aziz himself dreams of Islamic conquest – out of which some good may come. Thus the ending of the novel perfectly embodies Forster's liberal beliefs.

I've constructed a working model of an answer for you here. It really doesn't matter whether you agree with it or not; what I hope it demonstrates is the need for any essay to work through a problem or discussion in a critical way, keeping to the question, drawing on evidence, and reaching some sort of conclusion that is in accord with that evidence. Let me try and summarise this section in a few points. A well constructed essay must have:

1 an opening paragraph that engages with the question;
2 subsequent paragraphs that develop an argument in response to the issues raised by the question, supported by detailed and accurate knowledge of the text;
3 a concluding paragraph that returns to the question and reconsiders it in the light of your discussion.

Preparing for an exam answer on Forster

The questions that you can be set on any author for an exam are really quite limited. There are only three or four big topics that are suitable. They will often be framed in terms of an antithesis but, however they are phrased, the response will rarely be one simple, straightforward answer. You need to think of the issues raised by your Forster novel, its structure and its characteristic use of language, as well as knowing the plot thoroughly and having detailed information on the characters. You also need to think about Forster's liberal world-view, the manner in which it shapes the novel's development and the solutions that it imposes. This way you will have a flexible response to any question that you are asked. As I suggested in my opening chapter, Forster has often been seen as something of a hybrid novelist, part social satirist, part visionary poet. Whatever novel you are studying, this is an important issue to be explored: what sort of style does he use in these two different modes? How successfully does he combine them? Does it matter if the work is rather uneven? What are the consequences of this double strategy for the characterisation – or for the text as a whole? . . . and so on. You must be able to demonstrate Forster's abilities as a social critic and humorist, as well as his use of symbolism and the other more mysterious, suggestive methods of writing that he employs.

If you are studying the early novels, the whole phenomenon of 'Sawston' is clearly an issue – what it stands for, and Forster's rather mixed feelings towards the values of his class. You need to be able to compare and contrast Sawston with Forster's treatment of Italy. Another relevant topic, and not only for the early novels, is the nature of Forster's morality and how satisfactorily it is worked out in the fiction. Is the privileging of personal relationships sufficient as a philosophy of life? Is it adequate, and can it bear the emphasis and weight that Forster puts on it? It is interesting to note that a novelist who appears to be quite charitable towards his characters can also be very ruthless in his judgements of them.

The rubric for *Howards End* is 'only connect' and you need to ask yourself how successful Forster is in his 'connections' in this particular novel. You might feel that he isn't very successful, but that this doesn't necessarily mean that the book itself is a failure because the strategies that Forster employs are inventive, instructive and artistically pleasing. If this is the novel you are studying, you need to have a good command of Forster's social analysis, understand his dilemma as a liberal with a social conscience, and the consequences of this for the text overall.

I suppose that *A Passage to India* is the novel that most commonly appears on exam courses. India itself will often feature in the questions that are set. You need to think about the challenge of Forster's Indian setting, how he uses it to test his characters and assumptions about Western civilisation generally. Another favourite question concerns the different levels in the work. Is it more successful, or best considered, as a political novel, or a symbolist, metaphysical one? Clearly this type of question invites you to discuss both aspects of the fiction, and then make some kind of judgement as to their relative success or failure. In as much as *A Passage to India* is the culmination of Forster's career as a novelist and draws upon many of his earlier themes, preoccupations and techniques, all the different angles and approaches that I've discussed in this section have relevance when you are preparing for an exam on this novel.

A final note on quotations

The ability to quote vast chunks of text indiscriminately is not an instant passport to success in an exam, nor will heavy reliance on quotation in an essay ensure that it is a good one. Nothing will annoy an examiner quicker than an essay packed with unhelpful or redundant quotations. On the other hand, skilful and discriminate use of the text will show an examiner that you know it well, and can select from it to support your argument. Quotation is invaluable as a quick and easy way of supplying evidence for your point of view, but it can never be a substitute for your own opinions. Always make sure that you are quoting for a reason, that it is the best quote you can find for the purpose, and that it is accurate. Keep quotes as short as you can, and make them work for you. By this I mean that there are very few occasions when a quote can just stand on its own without further comment; you need to put it in the context of your argument and use it either to confirm the point that you have just made, or as corroborating evidence for the point you are building up to. When you are quoting purposefully, the quotations that you use and the argument that you are developing should mutually support and explain one another. I always feel that learning long lists of quotations out of context is of dubious value; if you engage with the text meaningfully on your own terms, appropriate material will soon become familiar and significant to you. Then it is just a matter of making sure that you can write it down accurately. There's much less danger of quoting inappropriately or merely for the sake of it, because the material is now part of your reading and your understanding of the text.

One final word of advice. Quotations from the text, like the critical analysis of it by others, are useful aids for the student, but don't forget that the most interesting and valuable part of any essay is what you can bring to it yourself. You will write so much better if your opinions are your own, held out of conviction, rather than being passively absorbed from others. The purpose of this book has been to show you how to articulate your own response to a complex text by working through a number of graded stages and asking yourself a few simple questions. It's amazing how quickly you can build up material in this way. You will be in a better position to write good essays on Forster if you do – and still enjoy reading him afterwards.

Further reading

Books by Forster

All Forster's novels are available in excellent Penguin reprints of the definitive Abinger edition, and have scholarly introductions and notes. Besides novels, Forster wrote short stories and had a successful career as an academic and journalist. Other important writings which will help you, whatever novel you are studying, are also available in Penguin paperbacks. Those listed below are particularly recommended.

Aspects of the Novel (1927)
This started off as a set of lectures on the novel as a literary form. It is deceptively simple and straightforward, and will give you several ideas that are insightful into Forster's own methods as a novelist. These include his discussion of 'flat' and 'round' characters, 'pattern', 'rhythm' and 'prophesy'. It really is essential reading.

Abinger Harvest (1936) and *Two Cheers for Democracy* (1951)
These are collections of essays. If you read around in them you will get a good sense of Forster's wide ranging enthusiasms, interests and beliefs. I strongly urge you to read 'Notes on the English Character' in the first volume as background for Forster's satire on the middle class, and 'What I Believe', 'The Challenge of Our Time', and 'Art for Art's sake' in the second, for his views on politics and art.

Collected Short Stories (1947)
Forster's shorter fiction is very diverse; it forms an extension and supplement to his achievements as a novelist. This volume

contains those stories published in his lifetime. 'A Story of a Panic', 'The Eternal Moment' and 'The Road to Colonus' are key expressions of his philosophy of life.

The Life to Come and Other Stories (1972)
These are franker, uncensored treatments of class, race and sex not published until after his death. A reading of 'The Life to Come', 'The Other Boat', 'Dr Woolacott' and 'Arthur Snatchfold' will force you to revise your opinions of Forster and his capacities as a writer.

The Hill of Devi (1953)
This is a travel book on India and interesting background to *A Passage to India*, especially the Gokul Ashtami festival that forms the substance of the 'Temple' section. One can see the shift from documentation into art.

Books on Forster

1   Biography
Furbank, P. N.   *E. M. Forster: A Biography* (1974)
  (Humane, scholarly and exhaustive, this is the standard life.)

2   Early reviews and the reception of the novels on publication
Gardner, P. (ed.)   *E. M. Forster: The Critical Heritage* (1973)

3   Criticism: the establishment of a reputation (1940–70)
Trilling, L.   *E. M. Forster: A study* (1944)
  (The first major book by an important liberal critic. Still well worth reading.)
McConkey, J.   *The Novels of E. M. Forster* (1957)
  (A pioneer study helpful for the symbolic patterning in the novels.)
Beer, J.   *The Achievement of E. M. Forster* (1962)
  (Shows Forster's indebtedness to the Romantic poets.)
Bradbury, M.   *E. M. Forster: A Collection of Critical Essays* (1966)
Crews, F. C.   *E. M. Forster: The Perils of Humanism* (1962)
  (This places Forster in his liberal context.)

Gransden, K. W.   *E. M. Forster* (1962)
    (Still a good book for the beginner.)
Stone, W.   *The Cave and the Mountain* (1966)
    (This is an important study but, because of its psychoanaly-
    tical perspective, students should use it with caution.)
Thomson, G. H.   *The Fiction of E. M. Forster* (1967)
    (Stresses the Romance and anthropological aspects of the
    fiction rather than the social realism. A stimulating corrective
    but sometimes overstated.)
Wilde, A.   *Art and Order: A study of E. M. Forster* (1964)
    (Helpful on Forster's liberal aesthetics and their consequ-
    ence for the structure of the novels.)

4   Criticism since Forster's death
General Introductions for the beginner include:

Gardner, P.   *E. M. Forster* (1978)
Gillie, C.   *A Preface to E. M. Forster* (1983)
Martin, Sayre J.   *E. M. Forster: The Endless Journey* (1976)

There have been a number of specialist studies but, for the
    student, I think that the most valuable recent books are:

Colmer, J.   *E. M. Forster: The Personal Voice* (1975)
    (A helpful book for the general student who wants to learn
    a little more for it puts Forster in a wider historical context,
    and has the advantage of knowledge of unpublished material
    and the details of Forster's private life.)
Rosecrance, B.   *Forster's Narrative Vision* (1982)
    (Gives alert, close readings that concentrate on the rhetoric
    of the novels, especially the use of the narrative persona.)

Collections of essays on Forster:

Stallybrass, O. (ed.)   *Aspects of E. M. Forster* (1969)
Das, G. K. and Beer, J. (eds)   *E. M. Forster: A Human Exploration*
    (1979)
Hertz, J. and Martin, R. (eds)   *E. M. Forster: Centenary Revalua-
    tions* (1982)
    (The last two centenary volumes have useful annotated
    bibliographical surveys of the work done on Forster.)

5   Books on individual novels:
Howards End

Widdowson, P.   *E. M. Forster's Howards End* (1977)
   (Provides the social and political context for Forster's 'Condition of England' novel and shows how his liberal dilemma shapes the text.)

A Passage to India

Unsurprisingly, there is a wealth of material to help the student on this major novel. Useful basic books include:

Colmer, J.   *E. M. Forster: A Passage to India* (1967)
Ebbatson, R. and Neale, C.   *A Passage to India* (1989)

More detailed studies worth consulting for the critical and historical background:

Das, G. K.   *E. M. Forster's India* (1977)
Lewis, R. Jared   *E. M. Forster's Passages to India* (1979)
Levine, J. P.   *Creation and Criticism: E. M. Forster's 'A Passage to India'* (1972)
Parry, Benita   *Delusions and Discoveries: Studies on India in the British Imagination* (1972)

Collections of essays:

Beer, J. (ed.)   *A Passage to India: Essays in Interpretation* (1985)
Bradbury, M. (ed.)   *A Passage to India* (1966)
(*Macmillan Casebook* that contains part of the 1952 interview with Forster referred to in Chapter 7.)
Rutherford, A. (ed.)   *A Passage to India: A collection of critical essays* (1970)
(The more recent Beer collection is a valuable supplement but not a substitute for the earlier volumes which contain much important material.)